STECK-VAUG

CRITICAL T G

Reading, Thinking, and Reasoning Skills

Teacher's Edition

Authors

Don Barnes
Professor of Education
Ball State University; Muncie, Indiana

Arlene Burgdorf
Former Resource Consultant
Hammond Indiana Public Schools

L. Stanley Wenck
Professor of Educational Psychology
Ball State University; Muncie, Indiana

Consultant

Gloria Sesso
Supervisor of Social Studies
Half Hollow Hills School District; Dix Hills, New York

LEVEL

A	B	C	D	E	F

STECK-VAUGHN
COMPANY
A Subsidiary of National Education Corporation

TABLE OF CONTENTS

ISBN 0–8114–6609–4

1 2 3 4 5 6 7 8 9 0 PO 97 96 95 94 93 92

Teach critical thinking skills in 5 simple steps!

Steck-Vaughn Critical Thinking

CRITICAL THINKING

Up-to-date, exciting, and effective

- **Each unit focuses on one stage of *Bloom's Taxonomy!*** Each book addresses knowing, understanding, applying, analyzing, synthesizing, and evaluating. (Levels 1 and 2 focus on only the first four stages.)
- **Inviting new unit openers!** Arouse curiosity and lead students into units with a good attitude for learning.
- **Lessons address one skill at a time!** Students master each skill before they move on to the next.
- **"Extending Your Skills" section at the end of each unit!** Brief, two-page reviews provide a convenient mastery check.
- **Six-book sequential program!** Students' critical thinking skills improve as their reading level increases.
- **At-home blackline master for each unit!** Involves parents in reinforcing new knowledge.
- **Exciting presentation!** Students are motivated by the variety of new and challenging activities and current, level-appropriate illustrations.

UNIT 3 Applying

Applying means using what you kn... picture. How does ... her arms raised? ...ecial day? What ...o win the ... felt the way ...ny?

UNIT 1

BLOOM'...

KNOWLEDGE | COMPREHENSION | APPLICA...

UNIT 1: KNOWING

T-10

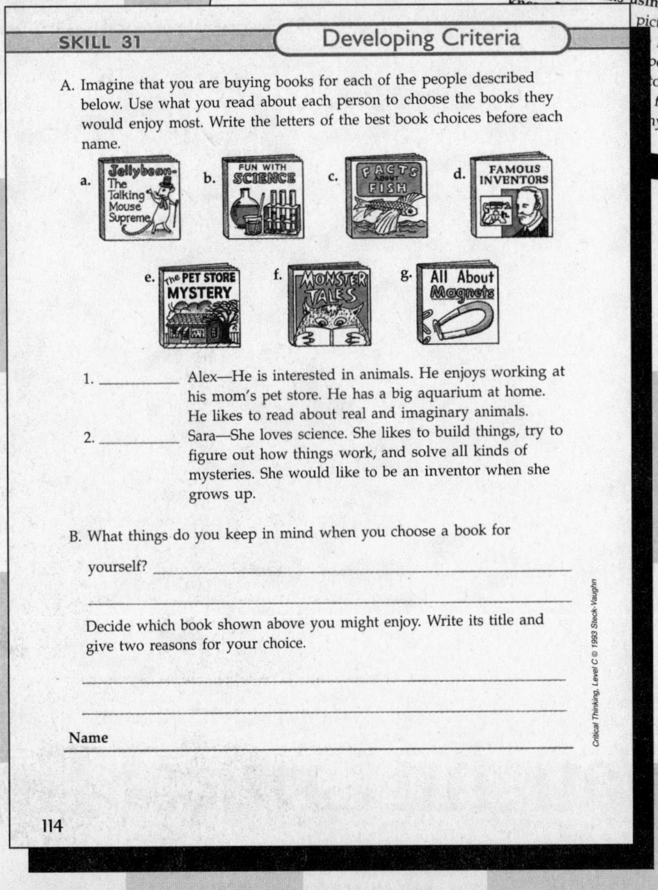

SKILL 31 **Developing Criteria**

A. Imagine that you are buying books for each of the people described below. Use what you read about each person to choose the books they would enjoy most. Write the letters of the best book choices before each name.

a. 

b. 

c. FACTS ABOUT FISH

d. FAMOUS INVENTORS

e. 

f. MONSTER TALES

g. All About Magnets

1. ________ Alex—He is interested in animals. He enjoys working at his mom's pet store. He has a big aquarium at home. He likes to read about real and imaginary animals.
2. ________ Sara—She loves science. She likes to build things, try to figure out how things work, and solve all kinds of mysteries. She would like to be an inventor when she grows up.

B. What things do you keep in mind when you choose a book for yourself? ________________

Decide which book shown above you might enjoy. Write its title and give two reasons for your choice.

____

Name ________________

114

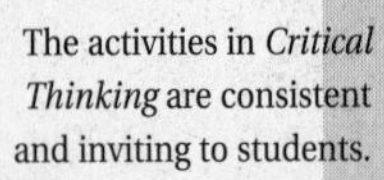

The activities in *Critical Thinking* are consistent and inviting to students.

Classifying

SKILL 1 PAGES 6–10

STEP ONE Define the Skill
Discuss with your pupils the meaning of *classifying*: **grouping things, people, or ideas because they are alike in some way.**

STEP TWO Identify the Steps
Explain to your students the steps they need to follow to classify any group of items, large or small:
1. Look at the items and decide which are alike in some way.
2. Place the like things together in one group.
3. Give a name to each group.
4. See if you can classify the items in one group into smaller groups.

STEP THREE Demonstrate the Skill
Ask pupils to watch and listen as you classify a group of items, following Step Two. **SUGGESTION:** On the board, write the names of different animals in random order. Then write three numbered categories—*pets, farm animals, wild animals*. Number animals by category, explaining why you are grouping them this way. Show pupils that one category may also be divided into smaller categories or be part of larger categories—for example, poodles and beagles are kinds of pet dogs; pet dogs, along with some pets, farm animals, and wild animals are furry animals.

STEP FOUR Practice the Skill
Use pages 6–10. See *Teacher Note* on each page.

STEP FIVE Provide Feedback
Discuss pupils' answers. **METACOGNITION:** Ask pupils to describe what they did. You may need to ask: **How did you decide whether certain things were alike? What did you look at or think about? How did you decide what name to give each group?**

ENRICHMENT ACTIVITIES

Present several categories, such as things that have wheels and things that grow. Challenge groups of pupils to list as many things for each category as they can in a certain amount of time.

Have pupils build a word web indicating how an item such as scissors may be used. Angled out from the word *scissors* might be *haircut, surgery, sewing*, and *cut paper*.

Classify animals according to where they might live. Help pupils conclude that some animals may live in several different areas. A horse might be at a circus, on a farm, or in the wild; a snake might be on a farm and in a jungle.

Real and Fanciful

SKILL 2 PAGES 11–12

STEP ONE Define the Skill
Discuss with your pupils the meaning of knowing the difference between *real and fanciful*: **knowing the difference between things that are real and things that are only imagined.**

STEP TWO Identify the Steps
Explain to your pupils the steps they need to follow to tell the difference between real and fanciful:
1. Look at a picture carefully or read the words carefully.
2. Decide whether the picture or the words tell about something that can really happen or something that can only be imagined.

STEP THREE Demonstrate the Skill
Ask pupils to watch and listen as you show the difference between real and fanciful, following Step Two. **SUGGESTION:** Write two sample sentences on the board—*My family lives in a brown brick house* and *My family lives in a magician's mirror.* Point out that the sentences are the same except for the final phrases. The last phrase in the first sentence describes a place where a family really could live; the last phrase in the second sentence does not. Therefore, the first statement could be real; the second is imaginary, or fanciful.

STEP FOUR Practice the Skill
Use pages 11–12. See *Teacher Note* on each page.

STEP FIVE Provide Feedback
Discuss pupils' answers. **METACOGNITION:** Ask pupils to describe what they did. You may need to ask: **How did you decide which things were real and which were fanciful? How did you decide which statements were real and which were fanciful?**

Knowing

TAXONOMY
ANALYSIS | SYNTHESIS | EVALUATION

...WLEDGE is the term used in Bloom's ...omy for the first stage in cognitive ...pment. This starting point includes both ...uisition of information and the ability ...l the information when needed.

...hors of this program have identified the ...g skills as being particularly helpful in ...ng Bloom's first stage:

...sifying
...iminating Between Real and Fanciful
...minating Between Fact and Opinion
...minating Between Definition and ...ple
...ing and Summarizing

...procedures for teaching each of these ... These lesson plans will help you use ...with ease as you incorporate *thinking* ...ur teaching day. Enrichment activities ...ny each lesson will help your students ...wly acquired thinking skills to a ...ations.

...has been completed, copy and ...chool-Home Newsletter on

New and expanded teacher editions include a comprehensive introduction to each unit. Lesson pages are level appropriate and include stimulating enrichment activities to challenge students in different ways.

Teach critical thinking skills in 5 simple steps

This is an all-new edition of *Steck-Vaughn Critical Thinking*, but one thing hasn't changed: the acclaimed 5-step lesson plan. This thorough, predictable instructional approach has helped thousands of students develop reading and reasoning skills that will serve them for a lifetime.

1 **Define the Skill**
Discuss the meaning of classifying with your pupils: grouping ideas, objects, or people according to things they have in common.

2 **Identify the Steps**
Explain to your pupils the steps they need to follow to classify any group of items, large or small.

3 **Demonstrate the Skill**
Ask pupils to watch and listen as you classify a group of items, following the four steps.

4 **Practice the Skill**
Use pages 6-10 to give pupils an opportunity to practice classifying

5 **Provide Feedback**
Have pupils correct and discuss their answers.

The 5-step lesson plan is back!

Bigger, better Teacher's Editions

- **At-home; enrichment activities!** Sixteen new pages per book include parent-involvement activities and three types of all-new enrichment activities.
- **Level-appropriate Teacher's Edition introductions!** Teachers can model lessons on an appropriate example at each level.
- **Comprehensive lesson plans!** Clarify instructional theories, goals, and mechanics.
- **Lessons written in conversational tone include examples which demonstrate each skill!** Teachers can present lessons right out of the book with minimal preparation.
- **Scope and Sequence charts!** Correlate skills to appropriate page numbers in each book.
- **Progress chart blackline master!** Allows teachers to record and monitor each pupil's achievements.

Thinker's Corner

SCHOOL–HOME NEWSLETTER

UNIT 4
ANALYZING

In the fourth unit of ***Critical Thinking: Reading, Thinking, and Reasoning Skills***, your child has been studying the following skills:

- judging completeness
- relevance of information
- abstract or concrete
- logic of actions
- elements of a selection
- story logic
- recognizing fallacies

This newsletter is designed to provide an important link between home and school. You can support your child's learning habits by asking what he or she has learned in school and by discussing papers brought home. You may also wish to do some of the activities suggested in this newsletter.

What's Missing?
Have your child work with judging completeness by asking him or her to trace a picture of an object but to leave something out, such as a wagon without a wheel. Then your child should ask other family members if they can find out what's missing.

Can You Draw an Idea?
Help your child distinguish between concrete and abstract things by asking him or her to draw a picture of each of ... *dream*. Ask which are concrete things and which are abstract things. It will probably be much easier to draw a picture of the concrete things, because they can be seen, heard, felt, smelled, and tasted. Abstract things, such as *love, idea*, and *dream*, are not easy to picture.

Does This Make Sense?
Have fun with discussing logic of actions by asking your child to think of silly things to do, such as taking a bath on Main Street or swimming in syrup. After each suggestion, ask your child why each statement may not make sense.

Who, What, When, Where, How?
You can help your child understand the elements of a story by talking about a book he or she has recently read. Example questions are:

- Who are the main characters in the story?
- What happened in the story?
- When and where did the story take place?
- How did the story end?

Commercial Alert
You can help your child recognize fallacies in commercials. The next time you see or hear a commercial that makes certain claims, discuss with your child what the commercial is trying to convince you of. For example, will eating a certain cereal or wearing a certain shoe make you as good as a certain sports star?

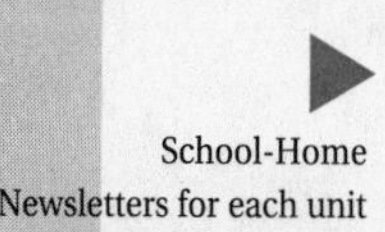

School-Home Newsletters for each unit include motivating At-Home activities that reinforce skills.

SCOPE & SEQUENCE

	Level A	Level B	Level C	Level D	Level E	Level F
UNIT 1 Knowing	**5**	**5**	**5**	**5**	**5**	**5**
Skill 1 Classifying	6–10	6–10	6–10	6–10	6–8	6–8
Skill 2 Real and Fanciful	11–14	11–14	11–12	11–12	9–10	9–10
Skill 3 Fact and Opinion	15–18	15–18	13–16	13–16	11–12	11–14
Skill 4 Definition and Example	19–22	19–22	17–20	17–20	13–14	15–16
Skill 5 Outlining and Summarizing	23–26	23–26	21–24	21–24	15–18	17–20
UNIT 2 Understanding	**29**	**29**	**27**	**27**	**21**	**23**
Skill 6 Comparing and Contrasting	30–32	30–32	28–30	28–30	22–24	24–26
Skill 7 Identifying Structure	33–34	33–34	31–32	31–32	25–26	27–28
Skill 8 Steps in a Process	35–38	35–38	33–34	33–34	27–28	29–30
Skill 9 Figural Relationships	39–40	39–40	35–36	35–36	29–30	31–32
Skill 10 Comparing Word Meanings	41–42	41–42	37–38	37–38	31–32	33–34
Skill 11 Identifying Main Ideas	43–46	43–46	39–42	39–42	33–34	35–36
Skill 12 Identifying Relationships	47–50	47–50	43–46	43–46	35–38	37–40
UNIT 3 Applying	**53**	**53**	**49**	**49**	**41**	**43**
Skill 13 Ordering Objects	54–56	54–56	50–52	50–52	42–44	44–46
Skill 14 Estimating	57–60	57–60	53–54	53–54	45–46	47–48
Skill 15 Anticipating Probabilities	61–64	61–64	55–58	55–58	47–48	49–50
Skill 16 Inferring	65–68	65–68	59–62	59–62	49–52	51–54
Skill 17 Changes in Word Meanings	69–70	69–72	63–66	63–64	53–56	55–56

	Level A	Level B	Level C	Level D	Level E	Level F
UNIT 4 Analyzing	**73**	**75**	**69**	**67**	**59**	**59**
Skill 18 Judging Completeness	74–76	76–78	70–72	68–70	60–62	60–62
Skill 19 Relevance of Information	77–80	79–80	73–74	71–72	63–64	63–64
Skill 20 Abstract or Concrete	81–84	81–84	75–76	73–74	65–66	65–66
Skill 21 Logic of Actions	85–88	85–88	77–78	75–76	67–68	67–68
Skill 22 Elements of a Selection	89–90	89–90	79–80	77–78	69–70	69–70
Skill 23 Story Logic	91–94	91–92	81–82	79–80	71–72	71–72
Skill 24 Recognizing Fallacies		93–94	83–86	81–84	73–76	73–76
UNIT 5 Synthesizing			**89**	**87**	**79**	**79**
Skill 25 Communicating Ideas			90–92	88–90	80–82	80–82
Skill 26 Planning Projects			93–94	91–94	83–86	83–86
Skill 27 Building Hypotheses			95–98	95–98	87–90	87–90
Skill 28 Drawing Conclusions			99–102	99–102	91–96	91–96
Skill 29 Proposing Alternatives			103–106	103–106	97–102	97–102
UNIT 6 Evaluating			**109**	**109**	**105**	**105**
Skill 30 Testing Generalizations			110–112	110–112	106–108	106–108
Skill 31 Developing Criteria			113–114	113–114	109–112	109–112
Skill 32 Judging Accuracy			115–118	115–118	113–116	113–116
Skill 33 Making Decisions			119–122	119–122	117–120	117–120
Skill 34 Identifying Values			123–124	123–124	121–124	121–124
Skill 35 Mood of a Story			125–126	125–126	125–126	125–126

CORRELATION TO CONTENT AREAS

	Level A	Level B	Level C	Level D	Level E	Level F
Reading and Language Arts	12, 13, 14, 15, 16, 17, 18, 22, 23, 26, 30, 34, 35, 36, 37, 41, 42, 43, 44, 45, 46, 51, 52, 55, 65, 66, 67, 68, 69, 70, 71, 72, 75, 79, 80, 83, 84, 88, 89, 90, 91, 92, 93, 94, 95, 96	7, 9, 11, 12, 13, 14, 15, 16, 17, 20, 21, 22, 24, 25, 27, 28, 32, 34, 35, 37, 41, 42, 43, 45, 46, 50, 52, 61, 62, 63, 65, 67, 68, 69, 70, 71, 72, 74, 78, 80, 82, 88, 89, 90, 91, 92, 94, 96	6, 11, 12, 13, 14, 15, 16, 25, 29, 30, 31, 32, 37, 38, 39, 40, 43, 44, 45, 46, 48, 55, 56, 57, 59, 60, 61, 62, 63, 64, 65, 66, 67, 68, 70, 72, 73, 74, 75, 77, 78, 79, 80, 81, 82, 83, 84, 85, 86, 87, 88, 93, 95, 96, 97, 98, 101, 102, 110, 112, 116, 117, 119, 120, 121, 122, 123, 124, 125, 126, 128	7, 11, 12, 13, 14, 15, 16, 19, 20, 21, 26, 30, 31, 32, 33, 36, 37, 38, 39, 40, 42, 44, 45, 48, 55, 56, 57, 58, 59, 61, 62, 63, 64, 65, 66, 67, 69, 70, 71, 73, 75, 76, 77, 78, 79, 80, 81, 82, 83, 84, 85, 88, 89, 95, 96, 97, 98, 99, 100, 104, 105, 106, 112, 113, 116, 117, 119, 120, 121, 123, 124, 125, 126, 128	9, 10, 11, 12, 13, 15, 16, 19, 23, 24, 25, 26, 27, 31, 32, 35, 37, 39, 42, 47, 48, 49, 50, 51, 52, 53, 54, 55, 56, 57, 58, 61, 65, 66, 67, 69, 70, 71, 73, 74, 75, 76, 77, 78, 80, 82, 83, 87, 88, 89, 90, 92, 93, 94, 97, 98, 99, 100, 102, 106, 107, 111, 112, 117, 120, 121, 122, 123, 125, 126, 128	6, 9, 11, 15, 16, 17, 18, 19, 20, 22, 25, 26, 27, 33, 34, 35, 36, 38, 39, 40, 42, 51, 52, 53, 55, 56, 58, 60, 62, 64, 66, 68, 70, 71, 73, 76, 78, 82, 88, 89, 95, 96, 102, 113, 115, 120, 123, 125, 126, 128
Social Studies	7, 8, 9, 10, 20, 25, 49, 54, 61, 76, 77, 78, 85, 87	6, 8, 10, 18, 23, 26, 31, 33, 38, 47, 48, 49, 64, 66, 77, 79, 81, 85, 86, 87, 90	7, 9, 10, 22, 23, 26, 28, 33, 35, 42, 47, 76, 90, 92, 100, 103, 104, 105, 106, 107, 108, 114, 115, 118, 127	6, 8, 9, 10, 24, 25, 28, 46, 50, 58, 72, 74, 86, 91, 92, 93, 101, 103, 115, 118, 122	7, 14, 15, 17, 28, 33, 36, 38, 44, 57, 60, 62, 63, 64, 68, 70, 81, 84, 85, 101, 113, 114, 116, 118, 119, 127	7, 12, 13, 14, 29, 30, 32, 35, 37, 41, 45, 50, 54, 57, 63, 65, 67, 69, 72, 74, 75, 83, 85, 90, 92, 97, 98, 99, 100, 101, 102, 108, 110, 112, 113, 114, 117, 118, 119, 121, 122, 123, 124
Science	6, 11, 19, 21, 24, 27, 28, 36, 38, 47, 48, 50, 62, 63, 64, 81, 86	19, 25, 44, 51, 64, 80, 93, 95	17, 18, 19, 20, 21, 23, 24, 34, 39, 41, 58, 90, 94, 99, 111, 113	17, 18, 22, 23, 29, 41, 43, 52, 90, 94, 107, 108, 110, 111, 114	6, 8, 18, 20, 22, 33, 34, 40, 72, 86, 91, 96, 103, 104, 108, 110, 115, 124	8, 10, 19, 24, 45, 46, 49, 61, 77, 80, 81, 84, 86, 87, 91, 93, 94, 98, 103, 106, 107, 116
Math	31, 32, 33, 39, 40, 54, 56, 57, 58, 59, 60, 74, 82	30, 36, 39, 40, 54, 55, 56, 57, 58, 59, 60, 73, 76, 83, 84	8, 36, 50, 51, 52, 53, 54, 71, 90, 91, 107	34, 35, 46, 47, 51, 53, 54, 60, 68, 90, 102, 109, 127	29, 30, 42, 43, 45, 46, 95, 109	21, 28, 31, 32, 44, 47, 48, 80, 94, 104, 109, 111, 120, 127

USING THE PROGRAM

Overview

Steck-Vaughn Critical Thinking is a six-book program designed to teach thinking skills. The skills are organized according to Benjamin Bloom's *Taxonomy of Educational Objectives.** At all six levels of the program, pupils are taught skills that have been identified as being particularly helpful in developing Bloom's first four stages of thinking—Knowledge, Comprehension, Application, and Analysis. At Levels C–F, pupils move into the higher-level skills of Synthesis and Evaluation.

Program Philosophy

Direct teaching of thinking skills provides pupils with the opportunity to focus on *thinking* rather than on specific content. Once pupils have begun to consider themselves "thinkers," they will be better able to learn and make use of content area material. *Steck-Vaughn Critical Thinking* is designed to help teach your pupils to think. This Teacher's Edition includes step-by-step lesson plans for teaching each of the thirty-five thinking skills which are found on pages T-10 through T-38 in this level.

Pupils need to practice newly acquired skills in order to retain them. Pupils who have had the opportunity to practice skills are better able to transfer them to other areas of the curriculum. *Steck-Vaughn Critical Thinking* contains practice pages for every skill presented in the program, as well as suggestions for enrichment activities.

Pupils need to know whether or not they are on the right track when they are practicing a new skill. Without feedback, a pupil might continue to practice a skill incorrectly. *Steck-Vaughn Critical Thinking* encourages the use of feedback. In addition, the program ties ***metacognitive skills*** to each lesson. Each lesson plan suggests questions to make your pupils "think about their thinking," as you discuss their responses to items on the practice pages.

Implementing the Program

The Scope and Sequence Chart on pages T-6 and T-7 of this guide identifies the skills taught in each level of *Steck-Vaughn Critical Thinking.* A complete lesson plan is provided for teaching each of these skills. Every lesson plan presents a five-step procedure that will help you use the program more easily:

STEP ONE: Define the Skill

In this step, you are given a definition that will help you explain the skill to your pupils.

STEP TWO: Identify the Steps

Here you are provided with concrete steps that your pupils can use as they learn the skill.

STEP THREE: Demonstrate the Skill

A suggestion is provided for demonstrating the skill to your pupils.

STEP FOUR: Practice the Skill

The pages developed for practicing the skill are listed for your convenience. In addition, each page in the text includes a ***Teacher Note*** that provides specific suggestions for using that page.

STEP FIVE: Provide Feedback

Questions are provided to help you get your pupils to "think about their thinking" (metacognition).

Each lesson plan also includes three suggestions for engaging pupils in meaningful enrichment activities. When your pupils can apply a new skill to material learned previously, they are demonstrating that they have truly mastered the new skill.

Involving the home in children's educational growth is of key importance. To encourage this involvement, School-Home Newsletters highlight the skills in the units and include activities that parents or guardians can do to reinforce the skills with their children.

The Class Assessment Summary is included for ease in tracking skill mastery by individual class members.

*Bloom, Benjamin. *Taxonomy of Educational Objectives, Handbook 1: Cognitive Domain.* New York: David McKay Company, Inc. 1956

UNIT 1

Knowing

BLOOM'S TAXONOMY

KNOWLEDGE	COMPREHENSION	APPLICATION	ANALYSIS	SYNTHESIS	EVALUATION

UNIT 1: KNOWING PAGES

KNOWLEDGE is the term used in Bloom's Taxonomy for the first stage in cognitive development. This starting point includes both the acquisition of information and the ability to recall the information when needed.

The authors of this program have identified the following skills as being particularly helpful in developing Bloom's first stage:

1. Classifying
2. Discriminating Between Real and Fanciful
3. Discriminating Between Fact and Opinion
4. Discriminating Between Definition and Example
5. Outlining and Summarizing

Step-by-step procedures for teaching each of these skills follow. These lesson plans will help you use the program with ease as you incorporate ***thinking skills*** into your teaching day. Enrichment activities that accompany each lesson will help your students apply their newly acquired thinking skills to a variety of situations.

After this unit has been completed, copy and distribute the School-Home Newsletter on page T-42.

SKILL 1 PAGES 6–10 Classifying

STEP ONE Define the Skill

Discuss with your pupils the meaning of *classifying:* **grouping things, people, or ideas because they are alike in some way.**

STEP TWO Identify the Steps

Explain to your students the steps they need to follow to classify any group of items, large or small:

1. Look at the items and decide which are alike in some way.
2. Place the like things together in one group.
3. Give a name to each group.
4. See if you can classify the items in one group into smaller groups.

STEP THREE Demonstrate the Skill

Ask pupils to watch and listen as you classify a group of items, following Step Two. **SUGGESTION:** On the board, write the names of different vehicles in random order. Then write three numbered categories—*land vehicles, water vehicles, air vehicles.* Number the vehicles by category, explaining why you are grouping them this way. Show pupils that one category may also be divided into smaller categories or be part of larger categories—for example, *cars and trucks are four-wheeled vehicles, which are used on land; some four-wheeled vehicles, along with some kinds of water and air vehicles, can be used to transport groups of people.*

STEP FOUR Practice the Skill

Use pages 6–10. See *Teacher Note* on each page.

STEP FIVE Provide Feedback

Discuss pupils' answers. **METACOGNITION:** Ask pupils to describe what they did. You may need to ask: **How did you decide whether certain things were alike? What did you look at or think about? How did you decide what name to give each group?**

ENRICHMENT ACTIVITIES

Display items such as a chalk eraser, chalk, magnet, pencil, and pen. Challenge pupils to classify the items. For example, the chalk eraser, chalk, and magnet are used with a chalkboard; chalk, pencil, and pen are used for writing.

Ask pupils to write a description of things that don't look alike but may be classified together in some way. For example, a knife, fork, and spoon look very different, but all are used for eating.

Pupils may enjoy classifying characters from a group of favorite stories, by role or personality.

SKILL 2 PAGES 11–12 Real and Fanciful

STEP ONE Define the Skill

Discuss with your pupils the meaning of knowing the difference between *real and fanciful:* **knowing the difference between things that are real and things that are only imagined.**

STEP TWO Identify the Steps

Explain to your students the steps they need to follow to tell the difference between real and fanciful:

1. Read the words carefully.
2. Decide whether the words tell about something that can really happen or something that can only be imagined.

STEP THREE Demonstrate the Skill

Ask pupils to watch and listen as you show the difference between real and fanciful, following Step Two. **SUGGESTION:** Write two sentences on the board—*We walked so far our feet hurt,* and *We walked so far our feet fell off.* Point out that the sentences are the same except for the final phrases. The last phrase in the first sentence describes what could really happen to your feet; the last phrase in the second sentence does not. Therefore, the first statement could be real; the second is imaginary, or fanciful.

STEP FOUR Practice the Skill

Use pages 11–12. See *Teacher Note* on each page.

STEP FIVE Provide Feedback

Discuss pupils' answers. **METACOGNITION:** Ask pupils to describe what they did. You may need to ask: **How did you decide which things were real and which were fanciful? How did you decide which statements were real and which were fanciful?**

ENRICHMENT ACTIVITIES

Use books such as *Charlotte's Web* and *Wind in the Willows* to demonstrate how the elements of fantasy in each story relate to everyday life. For example, the animals faced problems similar to those real people often experience.

Have pupils imagine a world of their own creation. Then have them contrast their imaginary world with the real world.

Have pupils write a realistic story about what they saw on their way to school. Then challenge them to write a fanciful version of the same event.

SKILL 3 PAGES 13–16 Fact and Opinion

STEP ONE Define the Skill

Discuss with your pupils the meaning of knowing the difference between *fact and opinion:* **knowing the difference between statements that can be proved true and statements that cannot be proved true.**

STEP TWO Identify the Steps

Explain to your pupils the steps they need to follow to know the difference between fact and opinion:

1. Read a sentence and decide whether it could be proved true. If it can be proved true, it's a fact.
2. Look for words such as *feel, think, best,* and *wonderful* in a sentence. They are clues that the sentence gives an opinion.

STEP THREE Demonstrate the Skill

Ask pupils to watch and listen as you show the difference between fact and opinion, following Step Two. **SUGGESTION:** Write two sentences on the board—*More people have pet cats than pet dogs,* and *Cats make better pets than dogs do.* Explain how the first statement can be proved true *(by looking it up in a reference book).* Explain how the second statement cannot; it also has a clue word that it is an opinion *(better).* However, caution pupils that opinions do not always have clue words.

STEP FOUR Practice the Skill

Use pages 13–16. See *Teacher Note* on each page.

STEP FIVE Provide Feedback

Discuss pupils' answers. **METACOGNITION:** Ask pupils to describe what they did. You may need to ask: **How did you decide a statement was a fact? How could you prove the fact? How did you decide a statement was an opinion? Were there words that gave you a clue?**

ENRICHMENT ACTIVITIES

Have pupils write statements that contain words such as *everyone, never, always,* and *all.* Encourage them to compare the validity of statements such as *Everyone thinks I'm funny* with *Most people think I'm funny.*

Pupils may enjoy writing ads containing facts and opinions. Encourage pupils to share their ads with the class. Then ask volunteers to decide which ads are factual.

Challenge pupils to find statements of opinion in an editorial or a letter to the editor in a newspaper or a magazine.

SKILL 4 PAGES 17–20 Definition and Example

STEP ONE Define the Skill

Discuss with your pupils the difference between *definition and example:* **the difference between knowing what a word means and naming things that belong to the group described by the word.**

STEP TWO Identify the Steps

Explain to your pupils the steps they need to follow to know the difference between definitions and examples:

1. Read each sentence or phrase and ask yourself, does it tell the meaning of a word? If so, it is a definition.
2. Ask yourself, does the sentence or phrase name things that belong to a group? If so, the names are examples.

STEP THREE Demonstrate the Skill

Ask pupils to watch and listen as you show the difference between a definition of a word and examples of the word, following Step Two. **SUGGESTION:** Write two sentences on the board—*A shoe is a covering for your foot*, and *Sneakers, sandals, and moccasins are kinds of shoes*. Point out the part in the first sentence that defines the word *shoe (is a covering for your foot)*. Explain that the words you listed in the second sentence are examples of the word *shoe*.

STEP FOUR Practice the Skill

Use pages 17–20. See *Teacher Note* on each page.

STEP FIVE Provide Feedback

Discuss pupils' answers. **METACOGNITION:** Ask pupils to describe what they did. You may need to ask: **How could you tell when you were reading examples? What did you do to match examples with definitions? How did you think of your examples?**

ENRICHMENT ACTIVITIES

Have pupils use magazines or newspapers to find examples of writing in which the writers have provided specific definitions of words. Discuss why writers might use this strategy.

Ask students if the definition "a game that's played on a field" is a good definition for *baseball*. Help pupils recognize that the definition could also apply to *soccer* or *football*. Invite pupils to suggest edits to improve the definition.

Point out that the meaning of a multiple-meaning word depends on its context. Have pupils name a multiple-meaning word, use it in a sentence, and identify the meaning that applies.

SKILL 5 PAGES 21–24 Outlining and Summarizing

STEP ONE Define the Skill

Discuss with your pupils the meaning of ***outlining and summarizing:*** **short ways of giving information. When you summarize, you tell only the main points. When you outline, you list the main points and details in an organized way.**

STEP TWO Identify the Steps

Explain to your pupils the steps they need to follow to summarize and outline:

1. Find the main idea—the most important idea in the paragraph or story.
2. Find the details—the information that helps explain the main idea.
3. To summarize, state the main idea in your own words. Leave out the details.
4. To outline, number the main ideas with Roman numerals. List details under each main idea and mark them with capital letters.

STEP THREE Demonstrate the Skill

Ask pupils to watch and listen as you summarize and outline, following Step Two. **SUGGESTION:** Select a story pupils have just read in their reading books. Summarize the story with a statement of the main idea. Then outline the story on the board, explaining how to mark main ideas and details with Roman numerals and capital letters.

STEP FOUR Practice the Skill

Use pages 21–24. See *Teacher Note* on each page.

STEP FIVE Provide Feedback

Discuss pupils' answers. **METACOGNITION:** Ask pupils to describe what they did. You may need to ask: **How did you find the main idea? How did you choose the facts, or details, that help support the main ideas? How did you know whether to put an idea after a Roman numeral or a capital letter in the outlines?**

ENRICHMENT ACTIVITIES

Provide pupils with a brief set of notes about a fire, such as those a newspaper reporter might scribble down while at the scene. Ask them to write a news article summarizing the event.

Offer pupils a list of topic sentences, such as *Dogs are lots of fun*. Ask pupils to write four additional sentences that provide supporting details about each topic.

Point out that words and phrases such as *early that day, afterwards, later*, and *just before going to bed* help us logically organize a summary. Ask pupils to summarize a recent day in their life by using similar groups of words.

UNIT 2

Understanding

BLOOM'S TAXONOMY

KNOWLEDGE	COMPREHENSION	APPLICATION	ANALYSIS	SYNTHESIS	EVALUATION

UNIT 2: UNDERSTANDING

COMPREHENSION is the term used in Bloom's Taxonomy for the second stage in cognitive development. Comprehension refers to the basic level of understanding and involves the ability to know what is being communicated in order to make use of the information. This includes translating or interpreting a communication or extrapolating information from a communication.

The authors of this program have identified the following skills as being particularly helpful in developing Bloom's second stage:

1. Comparing and Contrasting
2. Identifying Structure
3. Identifying Steps in a Process
4. Understanding Figural Relationships
5. Comparing Word Meanings
6. Identifying Main Ideas
7. Identifying Relationships

Step-by-step procedures for teaching each of these skills follow. These lesson plans will help you use the program with ease as you incorporate ***thinking skills*** into your teaching day. Enrichment activities that accompany each lesson will help your students apply their newly acquired thinking skills to a variety of situations.

After this unit has been completed, copy and distribute the School-Home Newsletter on page T-43.

SKILL 6 PAGES 28–30 Comparing and Contrasting

STEP ONE Define the Skill

Discuss with your pupils the meaning of ***comparing and contrasting:*** **looking at things to see how they are alike and how they are different.**

STEP TWO Identify the Steps

Explain to your pupils the steps they need to follow to compare and contrast two or more items:

1. Look carefully to see how the items are alike.
2. Look carefully to see how the items are different.

STEP THREE Demonstrate the Skill

Ask pupils to watch and listen as you compare and contrast a group of items, following Step Two. **SUGGESTION:** Present a list of sports—*baseball, basketball, football, soccer,* and *hockey.* Point out how they are all alike as members of a group—for example, they are all physical sports, and they are all played by teams. Point out the similarities between certain sports—for example, basketball and soccer are played with large balls; kicking the ball is important in both football and soccer. Then point out the differences—for example, baseball has untimed innings, while football has timed quarters; baseball is played on a diamond, while football, basketball, and soccer are played on rectangles.

STEP FOUR Practice the Skill

Use pages 28–30. See *Teacher Note* on each page.

STEP FIVE Provide Feedback

Discuss pupils' answers. **METACOGNITION:** Ask pupils to describe what they did. You may need to ask: **How did you decide that some things were similar and some things different? How did the pictures and words help you decide?**

ENRICHMENT ACTIVITIES

Have groups select a category, such as *mammals,* and list at least six examples and nonexamples. For example: *cows* and *whales* are mammals; *alligators* are not. Invite volunteers to read their list. Challenge the class to try to identify the category.

Explain that some words convey stronger mental images than others. Ask pupils to order words from the weakest to the strongest. Use the following groups of words: *enchanting, nice, acceptable; jog, walk, run; tap, hit, smash.*

Select pairs of unrelated words and ask students to list similarities and differences. Word pairs might include: *shoe/vase, computer/toaster, dog/book, song/ocean.*

SKILL 7 PAGES 31–32 Identifying Structure

STEP ONE Define the Skill

Discuss with your pupils the meaning of ***identifying structure:*** **finding out and describing how the parts of something are arranged and how together they help make up the whole thing.**

STEP TWO Identify the Steps

Explain to your pupils the steps they need to follow to identify the structure of something:

1. Look at the whole thing and tell what it is.
2. Look at the parts and list them.
3. See how the parts are arranged.
4. See how the parts together make up the whole thing.

STEP THREE Demonstrate the Skill

Ask pupils to watch and listen as you identify the structure of something, following Step Two. **SUGGESTION:** Draw or show a picture of a bicycle. Then identify the parts of the bike—*handlebars, frame, seat, pedals, chain, tires.* Note how the parts are arranged so that the pedals move the chain and the chain moves the tires, while the handlebars move to help steer the front wheel. Explain that all these parts together help make up the whole bike.

STEP FOUR Practice the Skill

Use pages 31–32. See *Teacher Note* on each page.

STEP FIVE Provide Feedback

Discuss pupils' answers. **METACOGNITION:** Ask pupils to describe what they did. You may need to ask: **How did you identify the parts of each whole? What helped you to understand their arrangement?**

ENRICHMENT ACTIVITIES

Have each pupil draw a picture of a building that is located nearby, without including the background or other identifying features. Challenge pupils to identify each building in the drawings by its structure alone.

Explain that paper models often are used to represent furniture within a room. The models may be moved to show possible arrangements. Challenge groups of pupils to make a schematic drawing of their classroom. Have them cut out and place furniture models within the drawing. Suggest that more able students try to make the furniture to the same scale as their drawing.

Display pictures or drawings of a variety of plants. As a class, examine and discuss the functions of the main structural parts *(leaves, stems, flowers, etc.)*.

SKILL 8 PAGES 33–34 Steps in a Process

STEP ONE Define the Skill

Discuss with your pupils the meaning of identifying ***steps in a process:*** **knowing the order of steps in a process and figuring out what comes next.**

STEP TWO Identify the Steps

Explain to your pupils the steps they need to follow to identify steps in a process:

1. Identify the end, purpose, or goal of the process.
2. Decide which steps are first and last.
3. Figure out the order of the remaining steps.
4. Check whether any steps are missing.

STEP THREE Demonstrate the Skill

Ask pupils to watch and listen as you identify the steps in a process, following Step Two. **SUGGESTION:** List in random order the actions needed to cover a book—for example, *fold the paper around the book, measure how much paper you'll need, tape the paper, cut the paper.* State the purpose or end result of the process—a covered textbook. Decide which steps are first and last. Number the remaining steps in order. Check to see whether any steps have been left out.

STEP FOUR Practice the Skill

Use pages 33–34. See *Teacher Note* on each page.

STEP FIVE Provide Feedback

Discuss pupils' answers. **METACOGNITION:** Ask pupils to describe what they did. You may need to ask: **How did you know which steps came first and which came last? How did you decide the order of the rest of the steps?**

ENRICHMENT ACTIVITIES

Display a picture showing a seedling growing in a flower pot. Give pupils sentences that tell in scrambled order the steps to follow when planting a seed. They can put the sentences in order to describe the process. Challenge pupils to make their own drawing showing a sequence of events.

Ask pupils to imagine they want to teach a friend to play checkers. Have pupils write the steps they would use to teach the game.

Challenge groups of pupils to research and report on the steps involved in specific animal activities. For example: a beaver building a dam, a chick hatching from an egg.

SKILL 9 PAGES 35–36 — Figural Relationships

STEP ONE Define the Skill

Discuss with your pupils the meaning of understanding *figural relationships:* **using figures to get information and to see connections between things.**

STEP TWO Identify the Steps

Explain to your pupils the steps they need to follow when using figures to get information and see connections:

1. Look at the whole figure to see what main information it gives.
2. Look at the parts of the figure to see the specific information they give you.
3. See how one part of the figure is related to another.

STEP THREE Demonstrate the Skill

Ask pupils to watch and listen as you use a figure to get information, following Step Two. **SUGGESTION:** Draw a simple bar graph on the board consisting of one main bar showing the months of the year. Ask pupils to tell you their birth month and include this information on the bar. Explain that the whole graph, or figure, shows how many pupils have birthdays in various months of the year. The graph also allows pupils to see in which months more of them have birthdays.

STEP FOUR Practice the Skill

Use pages 35–36. See *Teacher Note* on each page.

STEP FIVE Provide Feedback

Discuss pupils' answers. **METACOGNITION:** Ask pupils to describe what they did. You may need to ask: **How did you locate the parts in the figure? How did you decide what the figures where representing?**

ENRICHMENT ACTIVITIES

Obtain a catalog or brochure that shows signature rings and monogrammed pins. Encourage pupils to design a ring or pin that incorporates their own initials or names.

Ask pupils to work with a partner to make a bar graph representing the types of shoes their classmates are wearing.

Help pupils create their own secret code using a different symbol to represent each letter of the alphabet. Let students exchange secret messages with partners and decipher the message they receive.

SKILL 10 PAGES 37–38 — Comparing Word Meanings

STEP ONE Define the Skill

Discuss with your pupils the meaning of *comparing word meanings:* **seeing how words are similar or different in meaning and spelling.**

STEP TWO Identify the Steps

Explain to your pupils the steps they need to follow to compare word meanings:

1. Look at the word and pronounce it.
2. Decide what the word means.
3. Think of synonyms—words that mean almost the same thing.
4. Think of antonyms—words that mean the opposite.
5. See if you can add or drop letters to make a new word. See how this change also changes the meaning.

STEP THREE Demonstrate the Skill

Ask pupils to watch and listen as you compare word meanings, following Step Two. **SUGGESTION:** Show how much information the dictionary gives about word meanings by looking up the word *break.* Pronounce the word and read the meanings. Read or suggest synonyms and antonyms. Add or drop letters to create new words and meanings—*breakdown, breakfast*—and read those definitions from the dictionary also. Ask pupils to also list other words that have more than one meaning.

STEP FOUR Practice the Skill

Use pages 37–38. See *Teacher Note* on each page.

STEP FIVE Provide Feedback

Discuss pupils' answers. **METACOGNITION:** Ask pupils to describe what they did. You may need to ask: **How could you tell what each word meant? How did you think of synonyms? How did you think of antonyms?**

ENRICHMENT ACTIVITIES

Have volunteers enter words in a class word book. As a group, identify and enter a synonym and an antonym for each entry.

Ask pupils to copy a paragraph from a story, underlining several words to be replaced by synonyms. Have other pupils provide the synonyms and read the story aloud. Discuss how the meaning of the story was altered by the synonyms.

Ask pupils to think of two antonyms that have a common letter. For example, *lower* and *upper* are antonyms that have an *r* in common. Invite pupils to make a graphic design showing the two words connected by their common letter.

SKILL 11 PAGES 39–42 Identifying Main Ideas

STEP ONE Define the Skill

Discuss with your pupils the meaning of ***identifying main ideas:*** **knowing the main point in a paragraph or picture and noting how certain details tell about the main point.**

STEP TWO Identify the Steps

Explain to your pupils the steps they need to follow to identify main ideas:

1. Read the paragraph.
2. Decide what the main point is.
3. Find the main idea in a sentence or state it in your own words.
4. Note which details help tell about the main idea.

STEP THREE Demonstrate the Skill

Ask pupils to watch and listen as you identify the main idea of a paragraph, following Step Two. **SUGGESTION:** Write this paragraph on the board—*Some people have parties on their birthdays. They invite friends to help celebrate the day they were born. Their friends may bring presents. There may also be cakes with candles at birthday parties.* Read the paragraph. Note that birthday parties are the main point. Identify the sentence with the main idea—the first sentence. Note how the details in the other sentences tell about that point. Erase the first sentence and show how you can also tell the main point just by reading the sentences with details.

STEP FOUR Practice the Skill

Use pages 39–42. See *Teacher Note* on each page.

STEP FIVE Provide Feedback

Discuss pupils' answers. **METACOGNITION:** Ask pupils to describe what they did. You may need to ask: **How did you choose which words or sentence told the main idea? What kind of information did you get from the pictures?**

ENRICHMENT ACTIVITIES

Pupils may enjoy making a word web of things related to summer camp. Then they can decide on a main idea, make up details that support the main idea, and write a paragraph about summer camp.

Challenge pupils to identify the main idea in the following: *Potatoes have dents in their skin called "eyes." Actually the eye is a bud. These buds are important to the farmer. The bud is the part from which a new potato plant will grow.*

Challenge pupils to write a paragraph in which the details are arranged in order of importance. For example: *Weather can turn rocks into sand. Rain and wind does this. The tide hitting against rocks makes sand. Sand is tiny bits of rock.*

SKILL 12 PAGES 43–46 — Identifying Relationships

STEP ONE Define the Skill

Discuss with your pupils the meaning of ***identifying relationships:*** **seeing the connection between two or more things, ideas, or happenings.**

STEP TWO Identify the Steps

Explain to your pupils the steps they need to follow to identify relationships:

1. Read carefully. Think about the things or ideas you are reading about.
2. Ask yourself how these things or ideas are connected. Which things go together in groups? Which ideas belong with each other?

STEP THREE Demonstrate the Skill

Ask pupils to watch and listen as you identify relationships, following Step Two.

SUGGESTION: Write the following words and phrases on the board—*boathouse, heavy rain, breakfast, lake, lunch, flooding.* Read the words and phrases and pick the pairs that go together. Explain how they are related—for example, *boathouses are located on bodies of water such as lakes; heavy rain sometimes causes flooding; breakfast and lunch are both meals, with breakfast coming before lunch.*

STEP FOUR Practice the Skill

Use pages 43–46. See *Teacher Note* on each page.

STEP FIVE Provide Feedback

Discuss pupils' answers. **METACOGNITION:** Ask pupils to describe what they did. You may need to ask: **How did you connect ideas in your mind?**

ENRICHMENT ACTIVITIES

Have pupils report on the behavior of a particular animal. Challenge them to explain how the behavior may be related to the animal's survival.

Have pupils create relationships between ideas by writing sentences that use the words *so, therefore, because,* and *as a result.*

Have pupils identify the relationships in the following: *While Jack was studying, Kevin was watching TV. The next day, Jack sat next to Kevin in class. Jack had studied, so he did well on the test. Kevin did poorly.*

UNIT 3

Applying

BLOOM'S TAXONOMY

KNOWLEDGE	COMPREHENSION	APPLICATION	ANALYSIS	SYNTHESIS	EVALUATION

UNIT 3: APPLYING	PAGES
Skill 13 Ordering Objects	50 – 52
Skill 14 Estimating	53 – 54
Skill 15 Anticipating Probabilities	55 – 58
Skill 16 Inferring	59 – 62
Skill 17 Changes in Word Meanings	63 – 64

APPLICATION is the term used in Bloom's Taxonomy for the third stage in cognitive development. Application is the ability to use a learned skill in a new situation.

The authors of this program have identified the following skills as being particularly helpful in developing Bloom's third stage:

1. Ordering Objects
2. Estimating
3. Anticipating Probabilities
4. Inferring
5. Interpreting Changes in Word Meanings

Step-by-step procedures for teaching each of these skills follow. These lesson plans will help you use the program with ease as you incorporate ***thinking skills*** into your teaching day. Enrichment activities that accompany each lesson will help your students apply their newly acquired thinking skills to a variety of situations.

After this unit has been completed, copy and distribute the School-Home Newsletter on page T-44.

SKILL 13 PAGES 50–52 — Ordering Objects

STEP ONE Define the Skill

Discuss with your pupils the meaning of ***ordering objects:*** **putting items in order according to a pattern.**

STEP TWO Identify the Steps

Explain to your pupils the steps they need to follow to order objects:

1. Skim the items.
2. Determine the order the items should follow.
3. Decide which object is first and which is last.
4. Put the remaining objects in order between the first and last.

STEP THREE Demonstrate the Skill

Ask pupils to watch and listen as you order a group of objects, following Step Two. **SUGGESTION:** List the following words on the board—*city, state* or *province, village, country, town.* Tell pupils that you will order the items according to size—from smallest to largest. Identify the smallest—the village—and the largest—the country. Then place the remaining items in order—town, city, and state or province.

STEP FOUR Practice the Skill

Use pages 50–52. See *Teacher Note* on each page.

STEP FIVE Provide Feedback

Discuss pupils' answers. **METACOGNITION:** Ask pupils to describe what they did. You may need to ask: **How did you decide which item came first? Which came last? Is there another way you could arrange the items?**

ENRICHMENT ACTIVITIES

Have pupils rank the chores they do at home in order from the easiest to the hardest. Then have pupils write an explanation of their rankings.

Pupils may enjoy listing different TV programs and then ordering them from most favorite to least favorite.

Have pupils write a list of five things that are necessities and five things that are luxuries. Then have pupils number the items in order of personal importance.

SKILL 14 PAGES 53–54 — Estimating

STEP ONE Define the Skill

Discuss with your pupils the meaning of ***estimating:*** **using what you know to make a good guess.**

STEP TWO Identify the Steps

Explain to your pupils the steps they need to follow to estimate:

1. Picture the size, time, or amount of the things you are estimating.
2. Look for other facts you may need in order to estimate.
3. Use the picture in your mind and the facts to make a good guess.

STEP THREE Demonstrate the Skill

Ask pupils to watch and listen as you estimate, following Step Two. **SUGGESTION:** Standing near the front of the classroom, estimate the number of steps you are from the back of the room. Take one step and explain how you fix that distance in your mind. Then visualize the number you'd take to get to the back. Finally, walk to the back, counting off steps as you go. Emphasize the importance of imagining—or visualizing—when estimating.

STEP FOUR Practice the Skill

Use pages 53–54. See *Teacher Note* on each page.

STEP FIVE Provide Feedback

Discuss pupils' answers. **METACOGNITION:** Ask pupils to describe what they did. You may need to ask: **Could you picture what you were estimating? What else did you look at or think about to come up with a good estimate?**

ENRICHMENT ACTIVITIES

Pupils may enjoy estimating the measurements of various objects in the classroom and then using a measuring tape to determine the accuracy of their measurements.

Have pupils estimate how long they will take to complete an assignment. Then have them time themselves to see how close their estimate was.

Display a meterstick. Have pupils estimate the distance in meters between two objects. Then have them use the meterstick to check the accuracy of their estimates.

SKILL 15 PAGES 55–58 Anticipating Probabilities

STEP ONE Define the Skill

Discuss with your pupils the meaning of ***anticipating probabilities:* making a good guess about what will happen next.**

STEP TWO Identify the Steps

Explain to your pupils the steps they need to follow to anticipate probabilities:

1. Note all the facts that are given.
2. Think of things that might happen.
3. Guess which thing is most likely to happen.

STEP THREE Demonstrate the Skill

Ask pupils to watch and listen as you anticipate probabilities, following Step Two. **SUGGESTION:** Describe a situation—for example, *you plant some seedlings and place the pots in the window, but you forget to water them.* Think of what the plants may look like a week later—*green and lush, yellow and wilted, or brown and dead.* Predict which event is most likely to happen—*the seedlings will most likely be yellow and wilted.*

STEP FOUR Practice the Skill

Use pages 55–58. See *Teacher Note* on each page.

STEP FIVE Provide Feedback

Discuss pupils' answers. **METACOGNITION:** Ask pupils to describe what they did. You may need to ask: **What words did you use to guess what would happen next? Did you think of other things that might happen? How did you choose the one most likely to happen?**

ENRICHMENT ACTIVITIES

Read a short portion of a mystery story to the class and have pupils write a probable ending.

Have pupils write a story and remove the ending. Have them exchange stories with a partner. Pupils can then write endings to their partner's story and compare them with the original ending.

Have pupils tell how their lives might be different if they were living in a different part of the country.

SKILL 16 PAGES 59–62 Inferring

STEP ONE Define the Skill

Discuss with your pupils the meaning of ***inferring:* using information that is stated to come up with other information.**

STEP TWO Identify the Steps

Explain to your pupils the steps they need to follow to infer:

1. Note carefully all the pieces of information you are given.
2. Decide what information is missing (what you want to know).
3. Think of what else must also be true using the information you have.

STEP THREE Demonstrate the Skill

Ask pupils to watch and listen as you infer, following Step Two. **SUGGESTION:** Read the following paragraph aloud—*Mickey's mother walked* *into the kitchen. On the counter she saw a knife with peanut butter on it. An open jelly jar and a loaf of white bread sat next to it.* Note for pupils the information given—*the peanut butter, knife, jelly, and white bread.* Putting all that information together, infer along with Mickey's mother that Mickey made himself a peanut butter and jelly sandwich.

STEP FOUR Practice the Skill

Use pages 59–62. See *Teacher Note* on each page.

STEP FIVE Provide Feedback

Discuss pupils' answers. **METACOGNITION:** Ask pupils to describe what they did. You may need to ask: **What information did you use to infer your answer?**

ENRICHMENT ACTIVITIES

Have pupils read a fable. Ask them to infer how the basic message of the story might apply to their life at school.

Challenge pupils to describe the feelings of a character when they are not stated in the story. For example, read aloud *Tom's fishing pole and line pulled hard between his fingers.* Then discuss how Tom probably felt.

Have pupils write answers to questions. Ask volunteers to write a related question. For example, if the answer is *Go east two blocks to get to the train station,* the question was probably *Where's the train station?*

SKILL 17 PAGES 63–64 Changes in Word Meanings

STEP ONE Define the Skill

Discuss with your pupils the meaning of interpreting ***changes in word meanings:*** **knowing how a word can have different meanings depending on how it is used.**

STEP TWO Identify the Steps

Explain to your pupils the steps they need to follow to interpret changes in word meaning:

1. Look at the word. See if you can separate the word into meaningful parts.
2. Think of the most familiar meaning of the word.
3. Decide whether the familiar meaning is being used in this case.
4. If it is not, try to figure out the meaning based on the way the word is being used.

STEP THREE Demonstrate the Skill

Ask pupils to watch and listen as you interpret changes in word meanings, following Step Two. **SUGGESTION:** Write a sentence on the board—for example, *I think something fishy is going on here.* Note that the word *fishy* is *fish + y,* which can mean "like a fish." In this sentence, however, *fishy* doesn't have its usual meaning. Instead, *fishy* means "strange or suspicious."

STEP FOUR Practice the Skill

Use pages 63–64. See *Teacher Note* on each page.

STEP FIVE Provide Feedback

Discuss pupils' answers. **METACOGNITION:** Ask pupils to describe what they did. You may need to ask: **What sentence clues did you use to figure out the meaning of the word? What prefix clues did you use?**

ENRICHMENT ACTIVITIES

Demonstrate how the meaning of a word can change when applied to different items or ideas. For example, one meaning of *prime* is "first." A prime cut of meat is first quality meat; a prime minister is the top person in some governments.

List several words and see how many prefixes and suffixes pupils can add to the words to make new words.

Have pupils give as many synonyms as they can for the word *good.* Then have pupils identify differences in the meanings of the synonyms and how they would choose which synonym to use.

UNIT 4

Analyzing

BLOOM'S TAXONOMY

KNOWLEDGE	COMPREHENSION	APPLICATION	ANALYSIS	SYNTHESIS	EVALUATION

UNIT 4: ANALYZING

ANALYSIS is the term used in Bloom's Taxonomy for the fourth stage in cognitive development. Analysis is the ability to break down information into its integral parts and to identify the relationship of each part to the total organization.

The authors of this program have identified the following skills as being particularly helpful in developing Bloom's fourth stage:

1. Judging Completeness
2. Judging Relevance of Information
3. Judging Abstract or Concrete
4. Judging Logic of Actions
5. Identifying Elements of a Selection
6. Judging Story Logic
7. Recognizing Fallacies

Step-by-step procedures for teaching each of these skills follow. These lesson plans will help you use the program with ease as you incorporate ***thinking skills*** into your teaching day. Enrichment activities that accompany each lesson will help your students apply their newly acquired thinking skills to a variety of situations.

After this unit has been completed, copy and distribute the School-Home Newsletter on page T-45.

SKILL 18 PAGES 68–70 Judging Completeness

STEP ONE Define the Skill

Discuss with your pupils the meaning of *judging completeness:* **deciding whether something is missing from a picture or sentence.**

STEP TWO Identify the Steps

Explain to your pupils the steps they need to follow to judge completeness:

1. Look at the picture or read carefully.
2. Ask yourself if the picture or words make sense or if something is missing.
3. Complete the item by providing the missing part.

STEP THREE Demonstrate the Skill

Ask pupils to watch and listen as you judge the completeness of an item, following Step Two. **SUGGESTION:** Present the following situation (you may wish to write the particulars on the board)—*You receive a party invitation. On the invitation you are told the date of the party, the reason for the party, where the party is being held, and the fact that cake and ice cream will be served.* Point out that an important piece of information is missing—*the time of the party.* The invitation is therefore incomplete.

STEP FOUR Practice the Skill

Use pages 68–70. See *Teacher Note* on each page.

STEP FIVE Provide Feedback

Discuss pupils' answers. **METACOGNITION:** Ask pupils to describe what they did. You may need to ask: **How could you tell the item was incomplete? How did you decide what was needed to make it complete?**

ENRICHMENT ACTIVITIES

Have each pupil write an account of what happened in the classroom the previous day. Then have a partner judge the completeness of the account.

Give a problem and possible solution. Ask pupils to judge the completeness. *Problem:* More people came to the play than expected. *Solution:* Use chairs from another room. The problem statement does not state how many chairs are needed.

Ask pupils to draw a picture of a common object or scene that is familiar to the class. Have a partner judge the completeness of the picture.

SKILL 19 PAGES 71–72 Relevance of Information

STEP ONE Define the Skill

Discuss with your pupils the meaning of judging *relevance of information:* **deciding if an idea really matters to a topic or main idea, or if it is just extra, unneeded information.**

STEP TWO Identify the Steps

Explain to your pupils the steps they need to follow to judge relevance of information:

1. Identify the topic or main idea.
2. Find all the pieces of information given to you.
3. Decide whether you really need to know that information.

STEP THREE Demonstrate the Skill

Ask pupils to watch and listen as you judge relevance of information, following Step Two. **SUGGESTION:** Write a "Lost Dog" notice on the board. State the breed of dog, its approximate size and coloring, its name, the fact that it was the fifth puppy in a litter of five, a reward, and a phone number to call. Point out the various facts and note which one is irrelevant—the fact that the dog was fifth in its litter. A person does not need that information in order to identify and return the dog to its owner.

STEP FOUR Practice the Skill

Use pages 71–72. See *Teacher Note* on each page.

STEP FIVE Provide Feedback

Discuss pupils' answers. **METACOGNITION:** Ask pupils to describe what they did. You may need to ask: **How did you decide what information you needed to know? How did you decide what information was unnecessary?**

ENRICHMENT ACTIVITIES

Share an ad similiar to one from a newspaper lost-and-found section that says: *Large brown and white cat lost. Call 555–1472.* Challenge pupils to rewrite the ad, adding relevant information that might clarify the ad and help find the cat.

Make copies of an illustration from a book or magazine. Give pupils the copies and have them reconstruct the story from the illustration. Let each pupil contribute a sentence. Judge whether each sentence is or is not relevant to the story.

Display magazines such as *Cobblestone, National Geographic World,* and *Scouting*. Give pupils examples of subjects to research and ask which magazines on display would most likely have the information.

SKILL 20 PAGES 73–74 Abstract or Concrete

STEP ONE Define the Skill

Discuss with your pupils the meaning of deciding between *abstract or concrete:* **knowing the difference between things that can be seen or touched and things that can only be thought about.**

STEP TWO Identify the Steps

Explain to your pupils the steps they need to follow to decide between abstract or concrete:

1. Read the information.
2. Decide which items can be seen, touched, tasted, smelled, or heard. Put them in the concrete category.
3. Decide which items can only be thought about, such as feelings or ideas. Put them in the abstract category.

STEP THREE Demonstrate the Skill

Ask pupils to watch and listen as you show whether a term is abstract or concrete, following Step Two.

SUGGESTION: Write the following sentences on the board—*A girl can be almost anything she wants to be. Michelle wants to become a doctor*. Classify *girl* in the first sentence as abstract because the term refers to a general group. Classify *Michelle* in the second sentence as concrete because the name refers to a specific girl.

STEP FOUR Practice the Skill

Use pages 73–74. See *Teacher Note* on each page.

STEP FIVE Provide Feedback

Discuss pupils' answers. **METACOGNITION:** Ask pupils to describe what they did. You may need to ask: **How did you decide if something was concrete? How did you decide if something was abstract?**

ENRICHMENT ACTIVITIES

Have pupils create a list of general and specific words. For example:

	General	*Specific*
1.	furniture	table
2.	clothes	gloves
3.	insects	ants
4.	tree	evergreen
5.	vehicle	car
6.	book	dictionary

Challenge pupils to write about the meaning behind a symbol, such as the American eagle, a school mascot, the cross symbolizing the Red Cross, or the circles of Olympics.

Present a list of word pairs and ask pupils to identify which word is abstract and which word is concrete. For example, *building* is more abstract than *house.*

SKILL 21 PAGES 75–76 Logic of Actions

STEP ONE Define the Skill

Discuss with your pupils the meaning of judging the ***logic of actions:* judging if an action makes sense in a certain situation.**

STEP TWO Identify the Steps

Explain to your pupils the steps they need to follow to judge the logic of actions:

1. Figure out what the situation is.
2. Think of several actions you could take in that situation.
3. Choose the actions that make sense.

STEP THREE Demonstrate the Skill

Ask pupils to watch and listen as you judge the logic of actions, following Step Two. **SUGGESTION:** Present a situation to the class—*After school you go to the library with a classmate. When you are ready to leave, your classmate invites you to dinner. She lives five blocks south of the library, while you live five blocks north. You know you must ask permission from your parents.* List possible courses of action: *you can call from the library, you can call from your classmate's house, or you can walk home and ask.* Explain how the one action that makes sense is to call from the library.

STEP FOUR Practice the Skill

Use pages 75–76. See *Teacher Note* on each page.

STEP FIVE Provide Feedback

Discuss pupils' answers. **METACOGNITION:** Ask pupils to describe what they did. You may need to ask: **How did you decide which items made sense to use in each situation?**

ENRICHMENT ACTIVITIES

Have pupils write stories with an illogical element. Then ask volunteers to read aloud their story for classmates to identify the illogical elements.

Give examples of actions and ask pupils to decide on a logical reward. For example, *if John cleaned the playground for three months, should he receive a thousand dollars, a football, or a merit certificate?*

Present situations to groups of pupils and have them tell what they would do. Let the class discuss the logic of each group's action. Some sample situations: *You smell smoke in the house; you see a thief running from a store.*

SKILL 22 PAGES 77–78 Elements of a Selection

STEP ONE Define the Skill

Discuss with your pupils the meaning of identifying the ***elements of a selection:* identifying the parts of a story—the characters, setting, and action (plot).**

STEP TWO Identify the Steps

Explain to your pupils the steps they need to follow to identify the elements of a story:

1. Read the story.
2. Find the main characters—the people (or sometimes animals) in the story.
3. Note the setting—where the story takes place.
4. Describe the action that takes place—the plot.

STEP THREE Demonstrate the Skill

Ask pupils to watch and listen as you identify the elements of a selection, following Step Two. **SUGGESTION:** Select a previously read story from pupils' reading books. Name the main characters, note the setting or settings, and summarize the plot of the story.

STEP FOUR Practice the Skill

Use pages 77–78. See *Teacher Note* on each page.

STEP FIVE Provide Feedback

Discuss pupils' answers. **METACOGNITION:** Ask pupils to describe what they did. You may need to ask: **How did you figure out who the main characters were? How did you know where the story took place? How did you follow along with the action of the story?**

ENRICHMENT ACTIVITIES

Discuss a story set in the present day. Ask pupils how the plot, setting, and characters would change if the story took place 200 years ago.

Challenge pupils to write a description of a scene and a main character that is detailed enough for a partner to draw an accurate illustration for the story.

Read aloud several short stories and ask pupils to determine the author's purpose in each case. *Was it to entertain the reader? Was it to inform the reader? Was it to persuade the reader?*

SKILL 23 PAGES 79–80 Story Logic

STEP ONE Define the Skill

Discuss with your pupils the meaning of judging ***story logic:* knowing whether happenings within a story really have to do with the main idea and whether they follow the right order.**

STEP TWO Identify the Steps

Explain to your pupils the steps they need to follow to judge the logic of a story:

1. Determine the main idea of the story.
2. Ask yourself if each sentence really has to do with the main idea or if it gives information that does not belong or does not make sense.
3. Make sure the happenings are in the right order.

STEP THREE Demonstrate the Skill

Ask pupils to watch and listen as you judge the logic of a short paragraph, following Step Two. **SUGGESTION:** Write the following paragraph on the board—*Jenny and Mark brought Mark's kite to a big field. Jenny ran with the kite while Mark held the reel. Mark received a great new kite for his birthday. Soon the wind took the kite right out of Jenny's hands and sent it flying. Mark has brown hair and green eyes.* Explain that the main idea is flying Mark's kite. The third sentence should come first; it explains how Mark got the kite. The last sentence should be dropped; it doesn't belong because it doesn't have anything to do with flying the kite. Rewrite the paragraph correctly.

STEP FOUR Practice the Skill

Use pages 79–80. See *Teacher Note* on each page.

STEP FIVE Provide Feedback

Discuss pupils' answers. **METACOGNITION:** Ask pupils to describe what they did. You may need to ask: **What clues did you use to order the events? How did you identify ideas that did not fit?**

ENRICHMENT ACTIVITIES

See how pupils can link two ideas by adding additional information. For example: *Rain came down in torrents. José couldn't bail out the water fast enough.*

Assign a topic about which pupils will write a short story. Have them begin a new line for each sentence and then cut apart the sentences. Ask pupils to exchange strips of paper with a partner and organize the sentences to tell the story.

Discuss a character in a familiar story. Then ask pupils to suggest other actions the character might do—actions outside the story that would be consistent with the type of person the character is.

Recognizing Fallacies

STEP ONE Define the Skill

Discuss with your pupils the meaning of ***recognizing fallacies:*** **recognizing statements that are false.**

STEP TWO Identify the Steps

Explain to your pupils the steps they need to follow to recognize fallacies:

1. Read the statement carefully.
2. Decide if the statement is true.
3. If it is not true, decide why not.

STEP THREE Demonstrate the Skill

Ask pupils to watch and listen as you identify a fallacy, following Step Two. **SUGGESTION:** Write an *either/or* statement on the board—*On Saturday mornings, children either watch cartoons or sleep late.* Read the statement aloud and tell pupils it is incorrect. Point out why it is false—*children actually do many things on Saturday mornings, such as going to friends' houses, playing outside, cleaning their rooms.* Point out that the statement could be made true by making the following change—*On Saturday mornings, some children either watch cartoons or sleep late.*

STEP FOUR Practice the Skill

Use pages 81–84. See *Teacher Note* on each page.

STEP FIVE Provide Feedback

Discuss pupils' answers. **METACOGNITION:** Ask pupils to describe what they did. You may need to ask: **How did you determine that an analogy or a statement was false? How could you change it to make it correct?**

ENRICHMENT ACTIVITIES

Pupils might enjoy looking for fallacies in magazine and newspaper ads. For example: *You will be healthier if you eat this food.*

Give examples of sentences that generalize by using the words *always, best, everyone, nobody, worst.* Have pupils write sentences using each of these words. Then have pupils exchange papers and identify their partner's sentences as true or false.

Provide groups with a set of cards containing the following words: *bed, sleep, stove, cook, car, drive, ink, pen, lead, pencil.* Challenge pupils to use the words to make five fallacy-free analogies.

UNIT 5

Synthesizing

BLOOM'S TAXONOMY

KNOWLEDGE	COMPREHENSION	APPLICATION	ANALYSIS	SYNTHESIS	EVALUATION

UNIT 5: SYNTHESIZING PAGES

SYNTHESIS is the term used in Bloom's Taxonomy for the fifth stage in cognitive development. Synthesis is the ability to combine existing elements in order to create something original.

The authors of this program have identified the following skills as being particularly helpful in developing Bloom's fifth stage:

1. Communicating Ideas
2. Planning Projects
3. Building Hypotheses
4. Drawing Conclusions
5. Proposing Alternatives

Step-by-step procedures for teaching each of these skills follow. These lesson plans will help you use the program with ease as you incorporate ***thinking skills*** into your teaching day. Enrichment activities that accompany each lesson will help your students apply their newly acquired thinking skills to a variety of situations.

After this unit has been completed, copy and distribute the School-Home Newsletter on page T-46.

SKILL 25 PAGES 88–90 Communicating Ideas

STEP ONE Define the Skill

Discuss with your pupils the meaning of ***communicating ideas:*** **giving information to others in ways they can understand it.**

STEP TWO Identify the Steps

Explain to your pupils the steps they need to follow to communicate ideas:

1. Determine what you want to tell someone.
2. Choose a way to tell them.
3. Write the information on paper in the way you've chosen.

STEP THREE Demonstrate the Skill

Ask pupils to watch and listen as you model a way to communicate ideas, following Step Two. **SUGGESTION:** Present this situation to your pupils—*Your little sister asks you to explain what an elephant is. You begin to describe it in words—a large animal with a long trunk and big ears. Then you decide a picture would be even better, so you make a simple drawing of an elephant for her.* (You may want to draw such a picture on the board as an example.)

STEP FOUR Practice the Skill

Use pages 88–90. See *Teacher Note* on each page.

STEP FIVE Provide Feedback

Discuss pupils' answers. **METACOGNITION:** Ask pupils to describe what they did. You may need to ask: **How did you change the information from one form to another? Can you think of other ways to communicate this information?**

ENRICHMENT ACTIVITIES

Ask pupils to imagine that they are going away for several weeks. Have them write a letter to a friend who will take care of their pet. Tell them to make sure their friend understands the importance of following their instructions.

Display three posters headed *Casual, Formal,* and *Athletic.* Have pupils cut and paste photos from magazines onto the appropriate poster. Then have a class discussion about the ideas communicated by the photos.

Pupils may enjoy selecting photographs from magazines and communicating their reasons for choosing that photograph.

SKILL 26 PAGES 91–94 Planning Projects

STEP ONE Define the Skill

Discuss with your pupils the meaning of ***planning projects:*** **organizing time, materials, and effort to accomplish a goal.**

STEP TWO Identify the Steps

Explain to your pupils the steps they need to follow to plan a project:

1. Identify what you want to do.
2. Figure out the steps you need to take.
3. List the materials you need.
4. Figure out how much time it will take.

STEP THREE Demonstrate the Skill

Ask pupils to watch and listen as you plan a project, following Step Two. **SUGGESTION:** Present this situation to pupils—*You have to clean your room.* List on the board the steps that must be taken—*picking up and putting away clothes and toys, making the bed, dusting,* and *sweeping or vacuuming.* Next list the materials that would be needed—*dust cloth, broom,* or *mop.* Then estimate the amount of time each step would take.

STEP FOUR Practice the Skill

Use pages 91–94. See *Teacher Note* on each page.

STEP FIVE Provide Feedback

Discuss pupils' answers. **METACOGNITION:** Ask pupils to describe what they did. You may need to ask: **How did you decide which materials you needed?**

ENRICHMENT ACTIVITIES

Have small groups plan a bicycle safety program. Have them list questions that they need to answer as part of their planning. For example: *Who should be involved? What specific skills should be taught?*

To correspond with a social studies unit, have the class plan a time line. Ask pupils to decide on materials to be used, the design of the time line, the dates, places, and/or people to be included, and a work schedule.

Have pupils work in groups to plan and write an ad for a one-month summer recreational program for first graders.

SKILL 27 PAGES 95–98 Building Hypotheses

STEP ONE Define the Skill

Discuss the meaning of ***building hypotheses:*** **thinking of possible explanations for things that happen.**

STEP TWO Identify the Steps

Explain to your pupils the steps they need to follow to build a hypothesis:

1. Decide what information needs to be explained.
2. Find connections between what needs to be explained and what you know has happened in the past.
3. Suggest an explanation.

STEP THREE Demonstrate the Skill

Ask pupils to watch and listen as you build a hypothesis, following Step Two. **SUGGESTION:** Present this situation to pupils—*The hot, dry summer is coming to a close. It hasn't rained all summer, and you decide to go swimming in a nearby pond. The water only comes up to your waist. At the beginning of the summer, it came up to your chest. Based on what you know has happened in the past, you can list these possible explanations—someone has drained water from the pond, some of the pond water has evaporated and hasn't been replaced by rain, you've grown much taller.* What might be the most likely explanation?

STEP FOUR Practice the Skill

Use pages 95–98. See *Teacher Note* on each page.

STEP FIVE Provide Feedback

Discuss pupils' answers. **METACOGNITION:** Ask pupils to describe what they did. You may need to ask: **How did you decide on the most likely hypothesis? How did you think of possible hypotheses?**

ENRICHMENT ACTIVITIES

Let pupils form a hypothesis from information and change it as new information is added. For example: *There is candy in the store.* (It is a candy store, drugstore, grocery store.) *There are also aspirins.* (It is a drugstore, grocery store.)

Tell pupils that a particular object, such as a glove, has disappeared from the classroom. Have them suggest possible explanations for its disappearance.

Assign a mystery story for pupils to read. Have them list several hypotheses at a predetermined break points as they read the story.

SKILL 28 PAGES 99–102 Drawing Conclusions

STEP ONE Define the Skill

Discuss with your pupils the meaning of ***drawing conclusions:*** **using all the information you have to make a decision about a problem or situation.**

STEP TWO Identify the Steps

Explain to your pupils the steps they need to follow to draw a conclusion:

1. Identify the problem or situation.
2. Study the problem or situation carefully. Look at all the information you have about it.
3. Think of a general statement—a conclusion—that must also be true about the problem or situation.

STEP THREE Demonstrate the Skill

Ask pupils to watch and listen as you draw a conclusion, following Step Two. **SUGGESTION:** Write the following paragraph on the board—*After our hike, our shirts were soaked with sweat. We drank a whole pitcher of lemonade. "Before you go on a hike again," said Mr. Cook, "you should remember to bring one of the most important pieces of equipment a hiker needs—a canteen of water."* Explain that all the facts in the paragraph describe a situation about a hike—*sweaty shirts, extremely thirsty hikers, and the need for a canteen.* From these pieces of information you can draw the conclusion that hikers should always bring along a canteen of water, but these hikers did not.

STEP FOUR Practice the Skill

Use pages 99–102. See *Teacher Note* on each page.

STEP FIVE Provide Feedback

Discuss pupils' answers. **METACOGNITION:** Ask pupils to describe what they did. You may need to ask: **Why did you draw the conclusions that you did? What facts did you consider when you were drawing your conclusions?**

ENRICHMENT ACTIVITIES

Challenge students to identify conclusions that can be drawn from short statements. For example: *Six houses on John's block are blue, three are white, and one is yellow.* Tell pupils that a likely conclusion would be that blue is the most popular house color on John's street.

Point out that scientists draw conclusions. The discoverer of penicillin, Alexander Fleming, left a dish of deadly germs by a window. Particles of mold blew onto the dish and later, some germs had been destroyed. Ask what Fleming concluded.

Pupils may enjoy holding a discussion about a movie and drawing conclusions about the plot or characters.

SKILL 29 PAGES 103–106 Proposing Alternatives

STEP ONE Define the Skill

Discuss with your pupils the meaning of ***proposing alternatives:*** **suggesting possible solutions to a problem.**

STEP TWO Identify the Steps

Explain to your pupils the steps they need to follow to propose alternatives:

1. Identify the problem.
2. Think of as many possible solutions as you can.

STEP THREE Demonstrate the Skill

Ask pupils to watch and listen as you propose alternatives for solving a problem, following Step Two. **SUGGESTION:** Ask pupils to imagine they are with a friend on their bikes, riding to the store. As they turn down a street, they see it is almost covered with water, but they cannot tell how deep it is. Propose several alternative solutions—*going home, trying to ride through the water,* or *turning around and trying another street.*

STEP FOUR Practice the Skill

Use pages 103–106. See *Teacher Note* on each page.

STEP FIVE Provide Feedback

Discuss pupils' answers. **METACOGNITION:** Ask pupils to describe what they did. You may need to ask: **How did you think of different solutions? Why do you think each would work? How would you choose the best solution in each case? How did you think of different ways to use the items?**

ENRICHMENT ACTIVITIES

Discuss methods of communicating, such as writing, signing, and codes. Challenge pupils to think of alternate methods of sending information, such as blinking the eyes or tapping.

Present a situation in which pupils must find an alternate way to meet a responsibility. For example: *You are in charge of preparations for a Saturday party, but your mother is ill and can't be left alone. What can you do?*

Challenge pupils to write a story beginning that describes a problem but no solution. Pupils can exchange papers, propose solutions to the problem, select the best solution, and complete the story. Allow volunteers to read their story to the class.

UNIT 6

Evaluating

BLOOM'S TAXONOMY

KNOWLEDGE	COMPREHENSION	APPLICATION	ANALYSIS	SYNTHESIS	EVALUATION

UNIT 6: EVALUATING

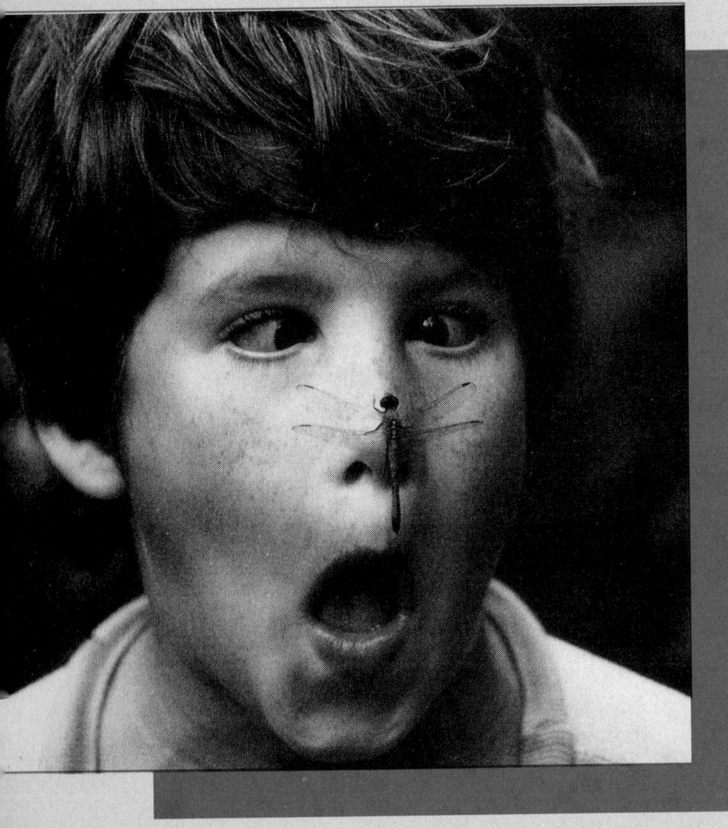

EVALUATION is the term used in Bloom's Taxonomy for the sixth stage in cognitive development. This final stage involves the ability to make a judgment about the value of something by using a standard.

The authors of this program have identified the following skills as being particularly helpful in developing Bloom's final stage:

1. Testing Generalizations
2. Developing Criteria
3. Judging Accuracy
4. Making Decisions
5. Identifying Values
6. Interpreting the Mood of a Story

Step-by-step procedures for teaching each of these skills follow. These lesson plans will help you use the program with ease as you incorporate ***thinking skills*** into your teaching day. Enrichment activities that accompany each lesson will help your students apply their newly acquired thinking skills to a variety of situations.

After this unit has been completed, copy and distribute the School-Home Newsletter on page T-47.

SKILL 30 PAGES 110–112 Testing Generalizations

STEP ONE Define the Skill
Discuss with your pupils the meaning of ***testing generalizations:*** **deciding whether a general statement is true all the time.**

STEP TWO Identify the Steps
Explain to your pupils the steps they need to follow to test a generalization:
1. Read the generalization carefully.
2. Look for evidence that will prove the generalization false.

STEP THREE Demonstrate the Skill
Ask pupils to watch and listen as you test a generalization, following Step Two. **SUGGESTION:** Write the following generalizations on the board—*All three-letter words have just one syllable.* Write some three-letter words on the board—*cat, ate, try,* and *add.* Explain that the generalization might be true, but you don't have enough evidence to be sure. Write some additional three-letter words on the board, including the word *icy.* Note that *icy* proves the generalization is not true. Explain that it takes only one piece of evidence to show that a generalization is false.

STEP FOUR Practice the Skill
Use pages 110–112. See *Teacher Note* on each page.

STEP FIVE Provide Feedback
Discuss pupils' answers. **METACOGNITION:** Ask pupils to describe what they did. You may need to ask: **How did you decide if a generalization was true? How did you choose the correct generalization? How did you think of ways to disprove generalizations?**

ENRICHMENT ACTIVITIES

Ask pupils to write a generalization based on the following information: *In the past ten years, one pupil from Central School, one pupil from South School, and four pupils from North School have won the county spelling bee.*

Have each pupil write ten generalizations that contain the words *all, always,* or *only.* Pupils can then exchange papers, test the generalizations, and write explanations for their decisions.

Pupils may enjoy bringing magazine ads to class and then deciding how best to test the generalizations that are stated.

SKILL 31 PAGES 113–114 Developing Criteria

STEP ONE Define the Skill
Discuss with your pupils the meaning of ***developing criteria:*** **thinking of rules to use in making judgments or decisions.**

STEP TWO Identify the Steps
Explain to your pupils the steps they need to follow to develop criteria:
1. Ask yourself what needs to be judged or decided.
2. Think of good rules that will help you judge or decide.
3. Follow the rules to make your judgment or decision.

STEP THREE Demonstrate the Skill
Ask pupils to watch and listen as you develop criteria, following Step Two. **SUGGESTION:** Present this situation to the class—You need to find a book to read and make a book report. List these rules on the board—*the book should be very interesting, it should be short enough to read in a week, it should be a mystery because that's the kind of book you enjoy best.* Next, list the titles of these three books on the board—*Encyclopedia Brown, Boy Detective,* 110 pages; *Best Tales of the West,* 250 pages; *The Story of Marie Curie,* 130 pages. Use the criteria to judge which book should be read.

STEP FOUR Practice the Skill
Use pages 113–114. See *Teacher Note* on each page.

STEP FIVE Provide Feedback
Discuss pupils' answers. **METACOGNITION:** Ask pupils to describe what they did. You may need to ask: **How did you use the rules, or criteria, to make your judgment? How did you think of your own criteria?**

ENRICHMENT ACTIVITIES

Ask pupils what criteria they would use to select a book to read to kindergartners during recess on rainy days.

Pupils may enjoy planning a trip to the moon. Have them develop and write criteria for judging which supplies should be taken.

Have a class discussion of the criteria a family of six—a mother, father, three sons and one daughter—might use when buying a house.

SKILL 32 PAGES 115–118 Judging Accuracy

STEP ONE Define the Skill

Discuss with your pupils the meaning of *judging accuracy:* **judging whether a statement is correct and exact.**

STEP TWO Identify the Steps

Explain to your pupils the steps they need to follow to judge the accuracy of a statement:

1. Figure out the main idea of what you are reading.
2. Check to see that each sentence makes sense by itself.
3. Make sure one sentence does not disagree with another.
4. Describe whether the words explain or describe things exactly.
5. Ask yourself where you can check to make sure the information is right.

STEP THREE Demonstrate the Skill

Ask pupils to watch and listen as you judge the accuracy of a statement, following Step Two. **SUGGESTION:** Write the following paragraph on the board—*The zoo was so crowded that there must have been a million people there. The bears were one of the most popular animals. Signs said not to feed the bears, yet many people were throwing marshmallows for them to eat. I could tell this doesn't really hurt the animals because they all looked healthy to me.* Identify the main idea—*a trip to the zoo.* Point out that the first statement is not exact. There may have been many people at the zoo, but a million is an exaggeration. The fourth statement is probably inaccurate. Just because a bear looks healthy does not mean it is.

STEP FOUR Practice the Skill

Use pages 115–118. See *Teacher Note* on each page.

STEP FIVE Provide Feedback

Discuss pupils' answers. **METACOGNITION:** Ask pupils to describe what they did. You may need to ask: **How did you decide one statement contradicted another one? How did you decide a word was not exact? How did you choose a source?**

ENRICHMENT ACTIVITIES

Provide newspaper ads. Some should be very specific about quality of items and cost; others should use words such as *more for your money* and *better buys.* Ask pupils to decide which ads are the most precise and accurate.

Display pictures of camping equipment. Then have pupils write brief but inaccurate descriptions of several pictures. Invite volunteers to correct the discrepancies.

Write a promotional news item about a nine-hour bus trip. Then show a bus schedule indicating that riders must wait one hour at one point to change buses. Help pupils recognize that the trip actually takes ten hours.

SKILL 33 PAGES 119–122 — Making Decisions

STEP ONE Define the Skill

Discuss with your pupils the meaning of ***making decisions:*** **choosing what to do after carefully considering all the facts.**

STEP TWO Identify the Steps

Explain to your pupils the steps they need to follow to make a decision:

1. Identify the situation or problem.
2. Think of possible actions you could take.
3. Use rules (criteria) to choose the best action.
4. Be prepared to explain why you made the decision you did.

STEP THREE Demonstrate the Skill

Ask pupils to watch and listen as you make a decision, following Step Two. **SUGGESTION:** Present a situation—*you are assigned to do a school project on the environment, but you don't know whether to do it on recycling or saving wildlife.* Offer possible things to do—*ask your teacher, put off the project until the topic "comes to you," go to the library to get some information on both topics.* Choose the action that makes the most sense—*perhaps going to the library to get information on both topics to see which interests you more.*

STEP FOUR Practice the Skill

Use pages 119–122. See *Teacher Note* on each page.

STEP FIVE Provide Feedback

Discuss pupils' answers. **METACOGNITION:** Ask pupils to describe what they did. You may need to ask: **What made you choose the action you did? How did you use rules (criteria) to choose your decision?**

ENRICHMENT ACTIVITIES

Have a class discussion about a current movie. Challenge pupils to tell how the movie might have ended differently if the characters had made different decisions.

Remind pupils that often other people's decisions affect their life. For instance, if their parents had decided to live elsewhere, the children might have attended a different school. Discuss other examples.

Ask pupils to write how their life might be different today if someone in history, such as George Washington or King Henry VIII, had made different decisions.

SKILL 34 PAGES 123–124 — Identifying Values

STEP ONE Define the Skill

Discuss with your pupils the meaning of ***identifying values:*** **recognizing a person's beliefs or feelings about what is right.**

STEP TWO Identify the Steps

Explain to your pupils the steps they need to follow to identify values:

1. Study the situation.
2. Ask yourself: What is the right thing to do in this situation?
3. If you are reading about another person, ask yourself: What does this person think is the right thing to do? Is it the same thing I would do?

STEP THREE Demonstrate the Skill

Ask pupils to watch and listen as you identify values, following Step Two. **SUGGESTION:** Write this paragraph on the board—*Maura was making valentines for her classmates. There was a new girl in her class whom she didn't really know. The girl had just started at Maura's school a few weeks earlier. Maura decided to make an especially nice valentine for her.* Show pupils how you can infer from Maura's actions that she believes we should be kind to other people. Kindness is a value that guided Maura's behavior.

STEP FOUR Practice the Skill

Use pages 123–124. See *Teacher Note* on each page.

STEP FIVE Provide Feedback

Discuss pupils' answers. **METACOGNITION:** Ask pupils to describe what they did. You may need to ask: **What clues helped you identify the values? Why did you choose the solution you did?**

ENRICHMENT ACTIVITIES

Have an election of class officers. Before the election, have pupils interview their classmates to find out what they look for in a candidate.

Present a situation in which a team is on the verge of a championship. The coach wants to send in a player who is weak. The player is moving out of town, and this is his last game. List reasons for and against letting the person play.

Ask each class member to clip one news item that represents a positive value and one news item that represents a negative value. As a group, read and discuss the items.

SKILL 35 PAGES 125–126 Mood of a Story

STEP ONE Define the Skill

Discuss with your pupils the meaning of identifying the ***mood of a story:*** **discovering the way the story makes you feel.**

STEP TWO Identify the Steps

Explain to your pupils the steps they need to follow to identify the mood of a story:

1. Look for words that help express a feeling.
2. Combine all these words to understand the kind of feeling the whole story has.
3. Ask yourself how the story makes you feel as you read it.

STEP THREE Demonstrate the Skill

Ask pupils to watch and listen as you find the mood of a story, following Step Two. **SUGGESTION:** Write this paragraph on the board—*With one strong kick, Glenda sent the soccer ball sailing into the net. The winning goal! The crowd cheered wildly. Her teammates leaped and whooped. Glenda beamed.* Note the words *winning*, *cheered*, *whooped*, and *beamed*. Explain how these words help create a mood of joy and excitement in the story.

STEP FOUR Practice the Skill

Use pages 125–126. See *Teacher Note* on each page.

STEP FIVE Provide Feedback

Discuss pupils' answers. **METACOGNITION:** Ask pupils to describe what they did. You may need to ask: **What words did you use to help you identify the mood?**

ENRICHMENT ACTIVITIES

Challenge pupils to think of descriptions a writer might use to convey a character's mood. For example, to show that a story character is nervous, an author might write that the character *squirmed in her seat.*

Read a selection to pupils. Then have them establish the mood and identify the clue words that led to their decision.

After reading aloud a story, urge pupils to discuss how the characters' actions in the story affected the mood of the story. Have pupils suggest events they might add to the story to change the mood.

Class Assessment Summary

TEACHER

SCHOOL GRADE

Directions: Daily observation and planned activities help determine whether students have achieved mastery of a particular skill. Indicate each student's mastery of a skill by writing the date in the corresponding box.

	UNIT 1: KNOWING					UNIT 2: UNDERSTANDING						
	Classifying	Real and Fanciful	Fact and Opinion	Definition and Example	Outlining and Summarizing	Comparing and Contrasting	Identifying Structure	Steps in a Process	Figural Relationships	Comparing Word Meanings	Identifying Main Ideas	Identifying Relationships
NAMES SKILLS ▸	1	2	3	4	5	6	7	8	9	10	11	12

Class Assessment Summary

TEACHER

SCHOOL **GRADE**

Directions: Daily observation and planned activities help determine whether students have achieved mastery of a particular skill. Indicate each student's mastery of a skill by writing the date in the corresponding box.

	UNIT 3: APPLYING					UNIT 4: ANALYZING						
	Ordering Objects	Estimating	Anticipating Probabilities	Inferring	Changes in Word Meanings	Judging Completeness	Relevance of Information	Abstract or Concrete	Logic of Actions	Elements of a Selection	Story Logic	Recognizing Fallacies
NAMES / SKILLS ▶	13	14	15	16	17	18	19	20	21	22	23	24

Class Assessment Summary

TEACHER

SCHOOL GRADE

Directions: Daily observation and planned activities help determine whether students have achieved mastery of a particular skill. Indicate each student's mastery of a skill by writing the date in the corresponding box.

	UNIT 5: SYNTHESIZING					UNIT 6: EVALUATING					
	Communicating Ideas	Planning Projects	Building Hypotheses	Drawing Conclusions	Proposing Alternatives	Testing Generalizations	Developing Criteria	Judging Accuracy	Making Decisions	Identifying Values	Mood of a Story
NAMES SKILLS ▶	25	26	27	28	29	30	31	32	33	34	35

Thinker's Corner

SCHOOL–HOME NEWSLETTER

UNIT 1

KNOWING

In the first unit of *Critical Thinking: Reading, Thinking and Reasoning Skills,* your child has been studying the following skills:

- classifying
- real and fanciful
- fact and opinion
- definition and example
- outlining and summarizing

This newsletter is designed to provide an important link between home and school. You can support your child's learning habits by asking what he or she has learned in school and by discussing papers brought home. You may also wish to do some of the activities suggested in this newsletter.

Pack It

Help your child practice classifying by asking him or her to name some things you might pack if you were going on a camping trip (such as a tent, fishing pole, flashlight, and jacket) and which things you would take on a picnic (such as food, blanket, picnic basket, plates).

Real World Adventure

Check your TV listings to find a factual program, such as a program on space travel or animals in their natural habitat. Watch the program with your child. Discuss whether the information presented in the program is real or fanciful. Ask your child how scientists find out about space or about the life of animals in the wild.

Letter to the Editor

Along with your child, follow a local event or news item in your newspaper or on TV. Together with your child, discuss his or her opinion. You may even wish to help your child write a letter of opinion to the editor of the newspaper or the producer of the TV news.

A Word a Day

Each day post a word on the family bulletin board or refrigerator or message center. Choose a word from a newspaper, a magazine, or a book you are reading. Ask your child, as well as other family members, to find out what the word means. Encourage other family members to post words.

Tell Me About It

Help your child learn to summarize information by asking him or her to tell about a book he or she has just finished. A summary tells about the book in a few sentences. If your child gives too many details, ask for just the main ideas. If your child is too vague, ask for a few more details. Enjoy your child's story!

Thinker's Corner

SCHOOL–HOME NEWSLETTER

UNIT 2

UNDERSTANDING

In the second unit of *Critical Thinking: Reading, Thinking and Reasoning Skills,* your child has been studying the following skills:

- comparing and contrasting
- identifying structure
- steps in a process
- figural relationships
- comparing word meanings
- identifying main ideas
- identifying relationships

This newsletter is designed to provide an important link between home and school. You can support your child's learning habits by asking what he or she has learned in school and by discussing papers brought home. You may also wish to do some of the activities suggested in this newsletter.

Who, What, When, Where, How?

You can help your child understand the basic structure of a story by encouraging him or her to talk about a favorite story. Example questions are listed below.

- Who was the story about?
- What happened at the beginning of the story?
- What was the most exciting part?
- When and where did the story take place?
- How did the story end?

Clocks, Clocks, Clocks

Ask your child to draw a picture of three clocks that are in your house, such as a kitchen clock, a clock on a stove, a mantel clock, or an alarm clock. Then ask your child to compare and contrast the clocks by listing the ways they are the same and the ways they are different.

Make a Diamond Design

Encourage your child to make a design using only one shape, such as a diamond, triangle, or square. Perhaps the figures will form a scene. Perhaps they will be a design of large and small figures. Watch your child's creativity flow!

Just the Opposite

Play a game of opposites with your child. Write a word, such as *high.* Ask your child to write the opposite, such as *low.* Then give your child a turn to write a word with an opposite for you to identify. Have fun comparing word meanings.

The Bark in the Dark

Write a short story with your child. Suggest a story starter, such as *Late last night, the dog barked because* ____. Together, list what might have caused the dog to bark and choose the cause you like best. Then have your child further identify relationships by writing a short story to tell what happened.

Thinker's Corner

SCHOOL–HOME NEWSLETTER

UNIT 3

APPLYING

In the third unit of *Critical Thinking: Reading, Thinking, and Reasoning Skills,* your child has been studying the following skills:

- ordering objects
- estimating
- anticipating probabilities
- inferring
- changes in word meanings

This newsletter is designed to provide an important link between home and school. You can support your child's learning habits by asking what he or she has learned in school and by discussing papers brought home. You may also wish to do some of the activities suggested in this newsletter.

Birthday Book

Help your child practice ordering objects by suggesting that he or she make a birthday book of friends and relatives. Write names, addresses, and birth dates on 3" x 5" cards. Decide whether to order the names by alphabetical order or by birth dates. Your child may wish to make a cover for the book and staple the pages together.

How Long Will It Take?

Play an estimating game with your child. Ask him or her to estimate how long it will take to ride around the block or to eat a carrot. Then keep time while the activity is done and compare the estimate with the actual time. Choose other activities and do more estimating.

What's Going to Happen?

The next time you are watching a TV movie about a detective who has to solve a mystery, take time during the commercial break to ask your child some questions. You might ask *What do you think will happen next?* and *How do you think the detective will solve the mystery?* You and your child can have fun trying to anticipate what may or may not happen.

The Art of Detection

Detectives do a lot of inferring to identify the guilty party. Help your child practice inferring by making a list of clues, such as those listed below. Have your child explain who (or what) is the guilty party.

- Flower vase tipped over.
- Water spilled on table.
- Wet paw prints near vase.
- Cat licking paws.

What's the Difference?

Help your child identify differences in word meaning by asking:
What's the difference between . . .

- a scheduled meeting and an unscheduled meeting?
- an unexpected visitor and an expected visitor?
- a kept promise and a broken promise?

Thinker's Corner

SCHOOL–HOME NEWSLETTER

UNIT 4

ANALYZING

In the fourth unit of ***Critical Thinking: Reading, Thinking, and Reasoning Skills,*** your child has been studying the following skills:

- judging completeness
- relevance of information
- abstract or concrete
- logic of actions
- elements of a selection
- story logic
- recognizing fallacies

This newsletter is designed to provide an important link between home and school. You can support your child's learning habits by asking what he or she has learned in school and by discussing papers brought home. You may also wish to do some of the activities suggested in this newsletter.

Information, Please

Discuss relevance of information with your child by asking some important things to know before you buy groceries. For example, do you need to know where the grocery store is located (yes), do you need to know how many different kinds of canned vegetables they have (no), do you need to know what items you need (yes)?

A Ladder of Me

Help your child work with abstract and concrete words. Ask him or her to make a ladder, beginning with his or her name at the bottom, and gradually fill in more general terms to get to the broadest term of *living thing.* Example:

- Living thing
- Animal
- Mammal
- Human
- Person
- Boy
- John

You Decide

Read the first half of a story from a children's magazine such as *Highlights* to your child. Ask him or her to provide endings that contain logical actions based on what you've read.

Explain the Title

Titles of books or movies often try to get your attention, but they are also related to some event in the story. Help your child understand the elements of a selection by discussing the title. Ask your child to tell what the title of a book or a movie could mean. Ask what events in the book or movie are represented in the title.

Ad Search

Have your child look through old magazines to find several ads. Ask your child to look for fallacies in the ads. For example, *if someone wears a certain kind of basketball shoe, will his or her game improve? Why or why not?*

Thinker's Corner

SCHOOL–HOME NEWSLETTER

UNIT 5

SYNTHESIZING

In the fifth unit of *Critical Thinking: Reading, Thinking, and Reasoning Skills,* your child has been studying the following skills:

- communicating ideas
- planning projects
- building hypotheses
- drawing conclusions
- proposing alternatives

This newsletter is designed to provide an important link between home and school. You can support your child's learning habits by asking what he or she has learned in school and by discussing papers brought home. You may also wish to do some of the activities suggested in this newsletter.

Cn U Rd Ths?

Look through the classified ads of a local newspaper. Have your child make a list of some of the abbreviations used in the ads. What do the abbreviations stand for? Now encourage your child to use some of those abbreviations to write an ad.

Show Time!

A simple puppet show can be done with stick puppets and a shoebox for a stage. Ask your child to make a list of things that are needed for a puppet show project. For example, things needed to make the puppet might include paper, colored markers, yarn, glue, and craft sticks. Once the planning is done, you're ready to go to work!

Why Do You Think This Happened?

You can help your child build hypotheses by asking him or her to present at least two possible explanations for the following: *This morning you watered your flowers before school. However, when you came home, several of the flowers were missing. There are no footprints in the soil, nor is the soil disturbed. What could have happened to your flowers?* Possible explanations might be: birds took the flowers, someone stooped over to pick them but did not step in the soil. Then ask your child to explain the following: *There is water and mud all over the kitchen floor. It is not raining. In fact, it has not rained for a long time. It has gotten so dry that your dad has had to get out the hose and water the lawn. You know the lawn has been watered because you just walked across it. Where did the water and mud come from?*

Recycle, Reuse

Your child can practice proposing alternatives by suggesting new ways to use old things. For example, birdhouses can be made out of old milk cartons; egg cartons can be used to plant flowers. Encourage your child to think about some new uses for material that is recyclable.

Thinker's Corner

SCHOOL–HOME NEWSLETTER

UNIT 6

EVALUATING

In the sixth unit of ***Critical Thinking: Reading, Thinking, and Reasoning Skills,*** your child has been studying the following skills:

- testing generalizations
- developing criteria
- judging accuracy
- making decisions
- identifying values
- mood of a story

This newsletter is designed to provide an important link between home and school. You can support your child's learning habits by asking what he or she has learned in school and by discussing papers brought home. You may also wish to do some of the activities suggested in this newsletter.

Is This True?

You can help your child test generalizations by asking him or her to tell whether the following is true.

- A robin is a bird.
- A robin can fly.
- Therefore, all birds can fly.

Have your child explain why the generalization is not true and how it can be proved not to be true.

Planning an Outing

Ask your child to help plan a family outing or vacation by making a list of rules, or criteria, that your outing or vacation must meet! Have your child also set criteria for activities that include all family members.

You Decide

You can help your child practice decision-making by asking him or her to tell what he or she would do in the following situation: *Your sister wants a pet. She is allergic to fur, but she doesn't want a fish or a bird. She has lots of stuffed toys, and she wouldn't mind having more. You want to think of a unique pet. What could you give her?*

Identifying Values

Discuss family values with your child. Ask your child to tell about a time when he or she had to make a choice about doing something. What were the consequences of doing it one way as opposed to another? Ask your child what he or she would do if someone asked him or her to cheat on a test or to sneak into a stadium or theater without paying.

What Makes the Mood?

The next time you see a movie or TV program with an interesting mood, discuss what helps create that mood. For example, dark scenes, eerie music, and strange sounds can create a scary mood. Dancing characters, colorful sets, and light music can create a happy mood. Ask your child to tell how the movie made him or her feel.

NOTES

STECK-VAUGHN

CRITICAL THINKING

Reading, Thinking, and Reasoning Skills

Authors

Don Barnes
Professor of Education
Ball State University; Muncie, Indiana

Arlene Burgdorf
Former Resource Consultant
Hammond Indiana Public Schools

L. Stanley Wenck
Professor of Educational Psychology
Ball State University; Muncie, Indiana

Consultant

Gloria Sesso
Supervisor of Social Studies
Half Hollow Hills School District; Dix Hills, New York

LEVEL

A	B	C	**D**	E	F

STECK-VAUGHN
COMPANY
A Subsidiary of National Education Corporation

ACKNOWLEDGMENTS

Executive Editor
Elizabeth Strauss

Project Editor
Anita Arndt

Consulting Editor
Melinda Veatch

Design, Production, and Editorial Services
The Quarasan Group, Inc.

Contributing Writers
Tara McCarthy
Linda Ward Beech

Cover Design
Linda Adkins Graphic Design

Text:

Every effort has been made to trace the ownership of all copyrighted material and to secure the necessary permissions to reprint these selections. In the event of any question arising as to the use of any material, the editor and publisher, while expressing regret for any inadvertent error, will be happy to make the necessary correction in future printings.

Excerpt from THE PEOPLE, YES, copyright 1936 by Harcourt Brace Jovanovich, Inc.; renewed 1964 by Carl Sandburg. Reprinted by permission of the publisher.

Photography:

p. 5 — H. Armstrong Roberts
p. 14 — NASA
p. 27 — Nita Winter
p. 49 — Nita Winter
p. 67 — H. Armstrong Roberts
p. 87 — Nita Winter
p. 109 — H. Armstrong Roberts

Illustration:

pp. 6, 31, 94, 98 — Ruth Brunke
pp. 7, 29, 41, 53, 122 — Linda Hawkins
pp. 8, 17, 21, 37, 65, 79, 79, 84, 120, 126 — Barbara Lanza/Carol Bancroft & Friends
pp. 18, 19, 33, 39, 45, 52, 54, 57, 66, 70, 75, 77, 81, 85, 86, 91, 93, 97, 100, 110, 111, 113, 115, 117, 122, 124 — Lonestar Studio
pp. 24, 35, 60, 83, 107 — Scott Bieser
pp. 26, 28, 76, 121 — Liz Allen
pp. 42, 48, 55, 62, 73, 88, 103, 108, 114, 116, 123 — Jackie Rogers/Carol Bancroft & Friends
p. 51 — Nancy Walter

ISBN 0–8114–6603–5

 1 2 3 4 5 6 7 8 9 0 PO 97 96 95 94 93 92

TABLE OF CONTENTS

TABLE OF CONTENTS

UNIT 1

Knowing

Teacher Note
In order to develop Bloom's first stage—knowing—the pupil needs to engage in the following skills:

- Classifying
- Discriminating Between Real and Fanciful
- Discriminating Between Fact and Opinion
- Discriminating Between Definition and Example
- Outlining and Summarizing

Knowing means getting the facts together. Let's try it out. Look at the picture. What is the boy holding? Do you think he made the object? How can you tell? Look at the expression on the boy's face. What does it tell you?

Classifying

To **classify** means to group things that are alike in some way.

In some sports, an official game can only be played with five or more people. In other sports, you need only one or two people.

tennis	basketball	football	
soccer	fishing	golf	baseball

A. Write the name of each sport listed in the box under the proper heading.

Five or More People

1. football
   basketball
   baseball
   soccer

One or Two People

2. tennis
   golf
   fishing

B. Write the names of three sports that can be classified under the headings listed below. Answers will vary.

Played on a Court

basketball
volleyball
tennis

Played on a Field

football
baseball
soccer

Name ______________________

Teacher Note
Ask pupils to think of other sports that might be added to these classifications. Then ask them to think of other ways sports might be classified.

SKILL 1

Classifying

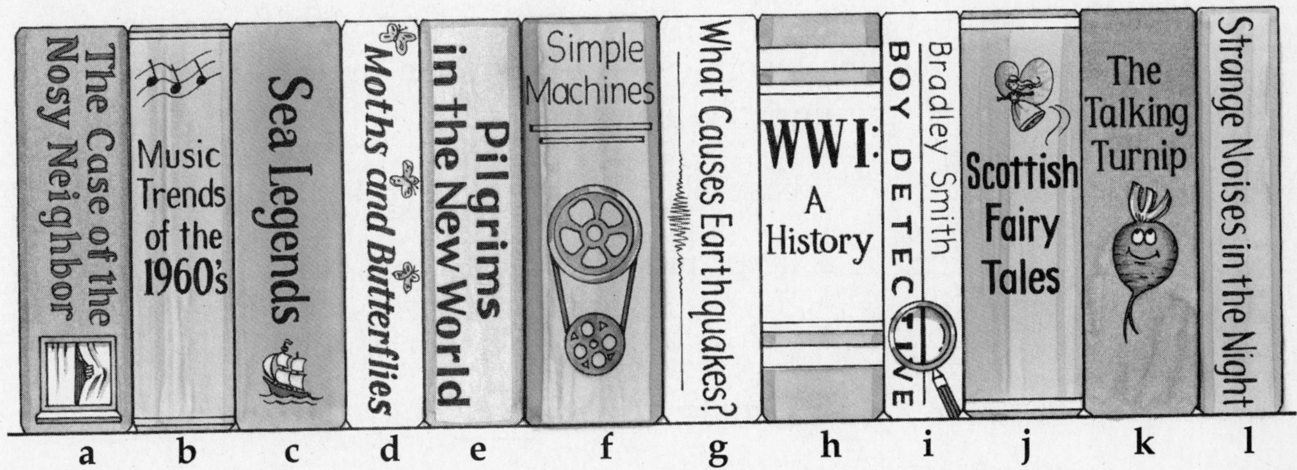

A. Bill's mother likes to read books about science, his brother likes to read mysteries, and his sister likes to read folklore. Write the letter of the books read by each member of Bill's family.

1. **Mother**	2. **Brother**	3. **Sister**
d	a	c
f	i	j
g	l	k

B. Read the book titles that have not been classified above. These books belong to Bill.

1. List the letters of the remaining books: b e h

2. What type of book does Bill like to read? history

C. What type of book do you like to read?

Answers will vary.

Name ________________________

Teacher Note
Ask pupils to name other types of books people might read. Write pupils' responses as headings on the chalkboard. Then have pupils make up titles for each category as you list them on the chalkboard under the correct headings.

Classifying

A. Circle the item in each group that does not belong with the other items. Then, on the line before each group, write the name of the group to which all the uncircled items belong.

toys ______ 1. baseball, rocking horse, (ruler), top, marbles

musical instruments ______ 2. harp, piano, clarinet, flute, (pillow)

clothes ______ 3. jacket, trousers, (nose), shirt, shoes

cities ______ 4. Toronto, Paris, (Brazil), Tokyo

workers (careers) ______ 5. (motor), baker, carpenter, plumber, tailor

B. Above the blanks are four words that could describe the objects listed. These words name some of the objects' possible characteristics. On the lines after each word, check the characteristics that might fit. (Some objects will have more characteristics listed than others.)

	Round	Colorful	Plaything	Sewed
1. baseball	a. ✓	b.	c. ✓	d. ✓
2. globe	a. ✓	b. ✓	c.	d.
3. marble	a. ✓	b. ✓	c. ✓	d.

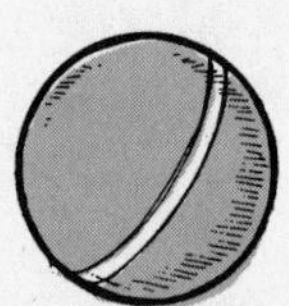

Name ______

Teacher Note
When pupils complete the page, ask them to suggest other items that could be included in each category. For part B, ask pupils to explain any answers that vary from those provided.

Classifying

A. Most of the words in the groups below have something in common. Some words are out of place. **First**, cross out two words in each list that do **not** belong. **Next**, write a word to name each group in the box above each list. **Last**, write each word that was crossed out below the group to which it belongs.

Dogs	Birds	Fish
poodle	wren	tuna
perch	cardinal	beagle
collie	bloodhound	trout
dove	canary	blue jay
Irish setter	herring	salmon
cocker spaniel	pigeon	bass
bloodhound	dove	perch
beagle	blue jay	herring

B. The words at the bottom of the page belong in three groups. Write the words on the lines below to make three groups. Then, give each group a name which fits all the items. The first name has been chosen for you.

Rivers	Trees	Continents
Nile	oak	Asia
Hudson	pine	North America
Amazon	birch	Africa
Mississippi	maple	Europe

Nile, oak, pine, Hudson, Asia, birch, Amazon,
North America, maple, Africa, Europe, Mississippi

Name ______________________

Teacher Note
After pupils have completed these exercises, ask them to add items to each list. You might make a game out of this by having one pupil call out a word in one of the six categories and asking the rest of the class to classify it.

SKILL 1

Classifying

A. Nine ways to group items are listed in the box. Write the group letter on the line before each item below. Find at least two group letters for each item. The first one is done for you.

a. made of wood	b. made of metal	c. a tool	d. a food
e. soft	f. made of cloth	g. made of clay	h. round
	i. long and narrow		

d, e, i 1. banana

a, b, c, i 2. spoon

a, b, c, i 3. yardstick

a, c, i 4. toothpick

a, b, g, h 5. ring

e, f, i 6. towel

b, c, i 7. saw

c, i 8. broom

b, c, i 9. needle

d, e, h 10. orange

a, b, g, h 11. pitcher

e, f, i 12. blanket

e, f, h, i 13. tablecloth

b, c, i 14. scissors

d, e, i 15. spaghetti

e, f, i 16. scarf

B. Decide how these items can be classified into three groups. Then, on the lines below, write the group names.

viper, lilies, Mexico, Japan, zinnia, cobra, Canada,
python, petunia, marigold, Cuba, boa constrictor

snakes ______ states ______ flowers ______

Name ______

Teacher Note
Explain to pupils that there are many ways of classifying an item. Point out that each item on this page can be classified in more than one way. After pupils have completed the page, discuss the various ways they classified each item and the reasons for their classifications.

Real and Fanciful

A. Write **R** before each sentence that tells something that could be real. Write **F** before each sentence that has a fanciful meaning.

1. R Santiago made up a story about a monster.

   F Santiago met a monster in the woods.

2. F The purple cow gave more milk than the white cow.

   R We read a poem about a purple cow.

3. F The dragon belched fire from its jaws.

   R Dragons are creatures in storybooks.

B. In each story below, underline the statement or statements that could be real.

1. Amparo was getting ready to fix the door that squeaked. She reached for a screwdriver, but the door reached out and grabbed it from her. "Wait," it said. "You don't need that. All I need is a little oil."

2. Jake was taking a walk in the forest. He saw a two-foot-tall man dressed in green standing beneath a tree. Jake picked up the little man and said, "Now, Mr. Leprechaun, you must lead me to your treasure!"

3. Chen gave his cat a bowl of milk. "No, thank you," said the cat. "I prefer water." Then the cat jumped up on the sink and lapped up some water from the dripping faucet.

4. A sea sprite sat on the rocks and watched Myra swim. Myra was scared and began to swim away. "Don't go," begged the sea sprite. "I only want to be friends."

Name ______________________________

Teacher Note
Begin by discussing the difference between real and fanciful, or make-believe. Review the answers with the class and discuss any misconceptions pupils have about what is real or fanciful.

Real and Fanciful

A. The quotes below are from a book called The People, Yes by Carl Sandburg. Each of the quotes is fanciful because it exaggerates the truth so much. On the line below each quote, rewrite the quote so that it is closer to reality. Answers will vary.

"They have yarns" . . .

1. "Of a skyscraper so tall they had to put hinges on the two top stories so to let the moon go by,"

   of a very tall skyscraper

2. "Of pancakes so thin they had only one side,"

   of extremely thin pancakes

3. "Of the herd of cattle in California getting lost in a giant tree that had hollowed out,"

   of huge giant redwoods

B. Place a check before the statements below that are fanciful.

√ 1. Because the beans grew so high, Dora had to climb them in order to touch their tops.

____ 2. Early in the morning, bison, elk, and deer came to drink from the pond.

____ 3. Many varieties of colored fish swam in the water.

√ 4. For his birthday, Jim got a poodle that could count.

√ 5. That evening after the performance, the circus animals discussed the audience.

Name ______________________________

Teacher Note
Be sure pupils know that "yarn" means tall tale in this context. If possible, get a copy of Sandburg's complete poem and read it to the class. Have pupils listen for additional exaggerations. Point out that poets and other writers often use fanciful language to make a point.

Fact and Opinion

Statements that can be proved true are called **facts**. Statements that describe only what someone thinks or believes are called **opinions**.

A. On the line before each fact sentence below, write **F**. On the line before each opinion sentence, write **O**.

O 1. It's (better) to have a picnic in the park than here.

F 2. There are thirty-six inches in a yard.

O 3. We (must) never plan a field trip on Friday.

F 4. More of the earth's surface is water than land.

F 5. Some clocks are run by batteries.

O 6. Our art class does (better) work than any other class.

F 7. In the 1400s, many people thought that the earth was flat.

F 8. A dozen is the same as twelve.

O 9. All books (must) be worth reading.

O 10. Everyone (should) take up aerobic dancing.

B. Certain words signal that an opinion is coming. Some examples are **should, better, must**. Find and circle these words in the sentences you marked **O** in exercise A. Then use these words to rewrite the following sentences and make them opinions. Answers will vary.

1. Students can learn how to play an instrument.

____

2. They can then play in the school band.

____

Name _______________

Teacher Note
Be sure pupils understand the difference between facts and opinions. After they complete part A, discuss why each answer is a fact or an opinion. Have pupils complete part B. Then discuss their opinion sentences. You might want to point out some phrases that signal opinions, such as *I think, I believe, I feel, in my opinion.*

Fact and Opinion

A. Write **F** on the line before each sentence that is a fact (a fact can be proved to be true). Put **O** on the line if the sentence gives someone's opinion. For each **O** sentence, circle the word or words which make you think that the sentence is an opinion.

F 1. Neil Armstrong was the first person on the moon.

O 2. Gloria's report on toads was (very well done.)

O 3. Being a pilot (must be) a dangerous job.

O 4. You (should) use red paint on your porch.

F 5. Thomas Edison invented the electric light.

O 6. (Everyone) likes pecan pie for dessert.

B. Rewrite the sentences from A. Write the fact sentences so that they express an opinion. Write the opinion sentences so that they tell a fact.

1. Answers will vary.
2. ______
3. ______
4. ______
5. ______
6. ______

Name ______

Teacher Note
After pupils complete part A, discuss their answers, particularly the words they circled. Note the words *must* and *should* in sentences 3 and 4. Point out that pupils could verify the facts in sentences 1 and 5. Have pupils complete part B, and then share their sentences with the class. Discuss the various sentences pupils write.

Fact and Opinion

Read the story below. On the lines below the story, write four facts and four opinions from the story.

A man, his son, and a donkey were traveling to market.

A farmer saw them and said, "You should be riding that animal." The boy got onto the donkey.

Soon, they met a group of men. "Lazy boy," one called, "you should let your father ride." The son got down and his father got on the donkey.

By and by, they met a woman who exclaimed, "You are mean. You should not make that boy walk." So the man took the boy up behind him.

Shortly, the travelers came to a village. Immediately, people began shouting, "Ungrateful wretches! That poor animal should not have to carry both of you." They both got off.

The man and the boy had a difficult time trying to decide what to do. Finally, they tied the donkey's feet together, put a pole between the donkey's legs, and carried the donkey.

Soon, someone along the road yelled, "I think that anyone would have to be stupid to carry a donkey."

The man and his son gave up in disgust.

Facts Answers may vary. Possible:

1. A man, his son, and a donkey were traveling to market.
2. The boy got onto the donkey.
3. Shortly, the travelers came to a village.
4. They both got off.

Opinions

1. Lazy boy, you should let your father ride.
2. You are mean. You should not make that boy walk.
3. That poor animal should not have to carry both of you.
4. I think that anyone would have to be stupid to carry a donkey.

Name ____________________

Teacher Note
Accept any factual sentences that pupils offer from the story for the facts. Discuss the opinion sentences pupils chose. Have pupils identify the words that made them select those sentences.

Read the news article. Then write a letter to the editor of the paper stating your opinion.

Will Wishton Become Wishing Wells?
Many Wish It Would; Others Wish It Wasn't So

If wishes come true, then the town of Wishton may soon change its name to Wishing Wells. A vote was taken by the city council last night to approve the name change. It is hoped that the new name would draw attention—and thus tourists—to the town's famous wishing well.

"People will come here from all over to see the well, toss in their coins, and make a wish," said council member Jim Hayes. "A new name will clear up any confusion about where that well is."

It is a well-known fact that many people now confuse Wishton with Wishington and never get here to see the wishing well. However, not everyone agrees with Mr. Hayes about changing the town name. "There's a lot more to this town than a wishing well," said Anna Riglio. "We've been known as Wishton for 150 years. I don't think we should change."

A demonstration for Wishton fans is planned for tomorrow afternoon at the wishing well.

Dear Editor:

Answers will vary.

Name

Teacher Note
Explain to pupils that they are to take a stand for either changing the town name from Wishton to Wishing Wells or keeping it as it is. Point out that a good letter to the editor offers facts to support the opinions given. Pupils may wish to make up additional facts to use in their letters. Have pupils share their finished letters, then discuss why some opinions are more convincing than others.

SKILL 4 Definition and Example

A **definition** gives the meaning of a word. An **example** is the name of an item belonging to the group. Several definitions and examples are listed below for the words **cat**, **fish**, and **bird**. Put **D** before the best definition at the left. Put **E** before the example at the right which fits.

I. cat:

_____ A. a member of the cat family

__D__ B. an animal with four legs, claws, a long tail, and fur

_____ C. a kitty which is kept for a pet

__E__ 1. Persian

_____ 2. Scottie

_____ 3. sparrow

II. fish:

_____ A. an animal that lives in water

__D__ B. a vertebrate that lives in water and has gills

_____ C. an animal covered with scales

_____ 1. turtle

_____ 2. frog

__E__ 3. trout

III. bird:

_____ A. an animal that flies

_____ B. an animal that lays eggs

__D__ C. a warm-blooded animal with feathers and wings that lays eggs

_____ 1. bee

__E__ 2. sparrow

_____ 3. butterfly

Name ______________________________

Teacher Note
Some pupils may need further clarification of definition and example before completing the page. Using item I as an example, point out that **A.** is too vague and **C.** is too specific to be a good definition. Ask pupils to give other examples for item I that would fit the definition (for example, calico, lion, tiger, panther, puma, cougar). Discuss pupils' answers to the rest of the page.

Definition and Example

A **definition** gives the meaning of a word. Read the definitions in group **A**. Look in group **B** to find the word that matches the definition. Write the letter of the word on the line before the definition. In group **C**, give two examples for each definition. The first one is done for you.

Examples will vary. Suggested:

A

c 1. material used in the body to sustain growth and provide energy

e 2. inner parts of the body that perform a special function

a 3. a woody plant with a long stem and deep roots

f 4. implements used in a kitchen to prepare food

b 5. devices used to produce sound

d 6. any way of exchanging information from one person to another

B

a. tree
b. musical instruments
c. food
d. communication
e. vital organs
f. cooking utensils

C

1. vegetables
   fruits
2. heart
   lungs
3. willow
   maple
4. skillet
   knife
5. piano
   guitar
6. speaking
   writing

Name ______________________

Teacher Note
Have pupils complete the first part of the page (matching *B* and *A*) before going on to *C*. Explain that the words in *B* are names for the definitions given in *A*. Pupils' answers to *C* will vary but should be legitimate examples. Have pupils share their answers so the class can appreciate the range of possibilities.

Definition and Example

To **define** a word is to give its meaning. A **fruit** is an edible (good to eat) product of a tree, bush, shrub, or vine. **Examples** of a word are illustrations of the kinds of items that belong to the group being defined. Apples, pears, bananas, and peaches are examples of fruits.

A. On the line before each sentence, write **D** if the sentence gives definitions. Write **E** if the sentence gives examples.

D 1. A mammal is an animal that gives milk to its young.

E 2. A rooster or hen is a fowl.

D 3. A bird which imitates the calls of other birds is the mockingbird.

E 4. Furniture refers to items such as beds, tables, or desks.

D 5. An emu is a large, three-toed Australian bird.

B. For each word, write a definition on line 1, and write at least two examples on line 2. You may use a dictionary. Answers will vary. Suggested:

a. **entertainer**
1. a person who entertains
2. comedian, dancer, singer

b. **book**
1. printed sheets of paper bound between covers
2. novel, history book, spelling book

c. **airplane**
1. a heavier-than-air craft that flies under power
2. jet, propeller-driven, (various brand names)

d. **teacher**
1. a person who teaches
2. reading teachers, (various levels and names)

Name ______________________

Teacher Note
Encourage pupils to use dictionaries to complete part B. Discuss the examples pupils give and whether they meet the criteria of the definition.

Definition and Example

Read the definition in each paragraph. Then write an example of your own on the lines. Answers will vary.

1. Friendship is the admiration and affection that two friends have for one another. In friendship, two people have an understanding and are willing to help each other out as well as share good times together.

   An example is

   ____

   ____

   ____

2. Courage is a quality that means someone has the strength to meet danger or hardship. Someone who has courage is firm of purpose and can overcome fear.

   An example is

   ____

   ____

   ____

3. A sense of humor has to do with someone's sense of fun. A sense of humor also has to do with someone's ability to see the wit and laughter in things.

   An example is

   ____

   ____

   ____

Name ____

Teacher Note
Suggest that pupils choose their examples from personal experience or something they have read. When pupils have completed the page, call on volunteers to share their examples. Discuss the variety of examples given.

SKILL 5 Outlining and Summarizing

A. Read each paragraph below. Then write two facts from the paragraph that support the main idea. Last of all, write each person's name under his or her mask.

Our class had fun with the paper-bag masks we made. One lunch hour we put on our masks and marched around the cafeteria. The other students loved it. Then we displayed our masks in the hallway.

Greg

Main Idea: Our class had fun with paper-bag masks.

1. We marched around the cafeteria in our masks.

2. We displayed our masks in the hallway.

Our masks showed great variety. Debbie's mask had a wide mouth and no hair. Jeff's mask had slanting eyes. Holly's mask looked like a girl wearing a headband, and Greg's mask looked sad.

Jeff

Main Idea: The masks showed great variety.

1. Answers will vary. Accept any two examples.

2. ______

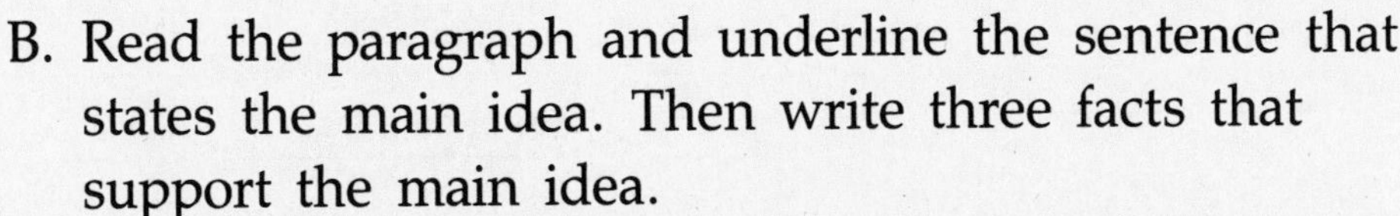

B. Read the paragraph and underline the sentence that states the main idea. Then write three facts that support the main idea.

Debbie

The ostrich is the largest living bird. An ostrich may be as much as eight feet (2.4m) tall and weigh three hundred pounds (135kg). Females lay eggs that weigh as much as three pounds (1.35kg).

1. It may be eight feet tall (2.4m)

2. It may weigh 300 pounds (135kg)

3. Its eggs may weigh three pounds (1.35kg)

Holly

Name ______

Teacher Note
Explain that outlining is a way to organize material. Have pupils complete part A. Point out that the organization of a paragraph is a main idea supported by details (in this case, facts). Have pupils complete part B. Then discuss how the fact sentences support the main idea.

Outlining and Summarizing

An **outline** is the frame or skeleton of a paragraph or an article. It shows how something is organized.

Fill in the outlines below. Follow the directions given for each part. Main topics have Roman numerals before them. Capital letters are used for subtopics.

A. Below are four main topics.

Ways of transporting coal
Formation of coal
Types of mines
Preparing coal

Write each main topic in a blank so that it fits the facts (subtopics) below it. The first one is done for you.

I. Formation of coal
   A. Plant life died
   B. It rotted
   C. Pressure was applied

II. Types of mines
   A. Surface
   B. Underground

III. Preparing coal
   A. Remove rocks
   B. Make pieces smaller
   C. Wash

IV. Ways of transporting coal
   A. Railroads
   B. River barges

B. Below are some facts (subtopics) about rabbits. Write the facts (subtopics) on the lines under the main heading each one fits.

Feed at night, Jackrabbit, Long ears, Kick and bite, Chisellike teeth, Cottontail, Strong hind legs

I. Appearance of rabbits
   A. Long ears
   B. Chisellike teeth
   C. Strong hind legs

II. Habits of rabbits
   A. Feed at night
   B. Kick and bite

III. Kinds of rabbits
   A. Jackrabbit
   B. Cottontail

Name ______________________

Teacher Note
Point out that pupils will first match an outline heading or main topic to the facts or subtopics that support it and will then match some facts or subtopics to main topics that are given.

Read the article below.

Planting a Garden

First, choose a spot of ground where plants will grow well. The ground should be fairly fertile. It should get plenty of sunshine. Pick a spot where you can bring water to the plants.

After you have chosen a garden spot, get the soil ready for planting. Scatter fertilizer over the ground. Next, dig up the ground and break up any large clumps of soil. Then, rake the soil until it is fine and the garden plot is level.

Now you are ready to plant some seeds. Dig the holes in straight rows. Place seeds an equal distance apart as the seed package shows. Cover the seeds with soil. Water the garden if rain does not come. Soon you should have some plants.

Follow these directions for making an outline.

1. Look at the first sentence of each paragraph to find the main idea. Write a main idea after each Roman numeral.
2. Write other facts on the lines below the main idea.
3. Begin each line with a capital letter.

I. Choose a proper growing spot
   A. Fertile ground
   B. Sunshine
   C. Water

II. Prepare the soil
   A. Scatter fertilizer
   B. Dig up ground
   C. Break up clumps
   D. Rake until level

III. Plant some seeds
   A. Dig holes
   B. Place seeds equally
   C. Cover with soil
   D. Water the garden

Name ____________________

Teacher Note
Tell pupils that it is not necessary to include every word in a sentence in an outline. Explain that they can summarize by using just the important words in the main idea sentences and for the facts in the subtopics.

Outlining and Summarizing

A **summary** is a restatement of the main points of a paragraph or an article.

Read the paragraph. Then complete the summary below it using key words from the paragraph.

The first handkerchiefs were used in ancient Rome. Only rich people could afford these white linen cloths, and they used them mainly for wiping their brows. When it became cheaper to make these cloths, ordinary Romans used them, too. They often waved their handkerchiefs as a way of greeting important people or applauding for actors in the theater. In later centuries handkerchiefs were very beautiful and were carried for display. Sometimes women gave a handkerchief to a man as a sign of affection.

Handkerchiefs were first used by early ___Romans___ of wealth to mop their ___brows___. Later, common citizens of Rome used ___handkerchiefs___ to ___wave___ at important people. In more recent centuries handkerchiefs were carried for ___display___ or given as signs of ___affection___.

Name ____________________

Teacher Note
Discuss the answers with the class. Some pupils may have chosen different words to complete the sentences, such as "forehead" for *brow* or "love" for *affection*. Ask pupils to compare the summary with the original paragraph to determine what was left out in the summary.

Extending Your Skills

A. Classifying

Read each quote and decide if it would have been said in the early 1700s or today. Write **past** or **present** on the line in front of each quote.

present 1. "I will do this assignment on my computer."

past 2. "Sarah is working at the spinning wheel."

present 3. "How do you like my new digital watch?"

past 4. "The town crier is calling out the news."

past 5. "It's Sebastian's turn to get water from the well."

past 6. "Becky forgot to take her hornbook to school."

present 7. "We'll tape that TV show so we can watch it later."

past 8. "The cooper said the barrel will be ready today."

B. Fact and Opinion

Study the picture. Then read the sentences. Put **F** before each statement of fact and **O** before each opinion.

F 1. The wig is white.

O 2. The wig is very elegant.

O 3. We should wear wigs like that today.

F 4. The wig is full and curly.

O 5. Wigs are better than hats.

F 6. The wig is for a man.

Name ______________________

Teacher Note
After completing the page, pupils may discuss and check their work with you or a partner.

C. Real and Fanciful

Read the story. Write an **R** above the pictures from the story that illustrate something that is real and an **F** above the pictures that illustrate something fanciful.

Caroline had been trying for some time, but she just couldn't get her kite to fly. The big white cloud floating above saw her and wanted to help. "I'll ask the wind to pick up her kite and make it fly," the cloud thought. But the wind was asleep and didn't like to be awakened. The cloud knew that if it upset the wind, the wind could blow it away.

"I know what I'll do," the cloud decided. "I'll ask the sun to wake up the wind. The wind always listens to the sun."

So the cloud spoke to the sun, and the sun woke up the wind. The wind blew just enough to make the kite fly but not enough to send away the cloud. Thanks to the cloud, the sun, and the wind, Caroline had great fun flying her kite.

R ______ F ______ F ______ R ______

D. Outlining and Summarizing

Write a summary of the story above. Use another sheet of paper if necessary. Answers will vary. ______________________________

____

____

____

Name ______________________________

Teacher Note
Review with pupils the meaning of the words *real* and *fanciful*. Point out that stories can be part real and part fanciful. Have pupils eliminate the fanciful parts of the story and tell it as a real story.

UNIT 2

Understanding

Teacher Note
In order to develop Bloom's second stage—understanding—the pupil needs to engage in the following skills:

- Comparing and Contrasting
- Identifying Structure
- Identifying Steps in a Process
- Understanding Figural Relationships
- Comparing Word Meanings
- Identifying Main Ideas
- Identifying Relationships

Understanding means telling about something in your own words. Look at the picture. What can you say about the two girls? Do you think they are friends? Why? What can you say about the baby? How do you know?

Comparing and Contrasting

A. To **compare** things means to tell what is alike about them. To **contrast** things means to tell what is different about them. Look at the pictures of the two bedrooms and read the paragraph. Identify Anita's room and Heather's room.

Anita and Heather both like to read. They both like to listen to the radio. Heather likes fancy things, while Anita likes things that have a simpler design. Anita lives in the city, but Heather lives in the country.

Anita's room   Heather's room

B. Use the information in the pictures and in the paragraph to answer these questions.

1. What else is the same about Anita and Heather?

   They both like apples.

   They both have goldfish.

2. How else are Anita and Heather different?

   Anita has a bird, and Heather has a cat.

   Anita plays tennis, and Heather skis.

Name ______________________

Teacher Note
Have pupils work in pairs to compare and contrast things about themselves. Then have them share their findings with the class to find their similarities and differences with other pupils.

Comparing and Contrasting

If you were to go back in time about 10,000 years, you might see some animals that look like the elephant of today. But you'd really be looking at mammoths and mastodons.

Mammoth

Mastodon

1. Compare and contrast the mammoth and the mastodon. How were the two animals alike? Answers will vary.

   They both looked like an elephant. They each had a trunk, tusks, and small ears.

2. Complete the table by telling how the two animals were different.

	Mammoth	**Mastodon**
Size	larger	smaller
Head	higher than hips	in line with hips
Tusks	curved upward and around	like those of an elephant

Name ____________________

Teacher Note
Have pupils re-examine the pictures and tell how each animal resembles the elephant. You may wish to show a picture of an elephant to your pupils so they can visually compare and contrast.

Comparing and Contrasting

A. On the lines below, explain how the items in each pair are alike.

Answers may vary.

1. snake and lizard both are reptiles
2. piano and harp both make music
3. clock and watch both tell time
4. book and magazine both are to be read
5. radio and television both entertain
6. roof and hat both cover something
7. sail and motor both move a boat
8. candle and bulb both give light
9. writing and talking both are forms of communication
10. bird and kite both fly

B. 1. Study the pairs in part A. In your opinion, which pair names things that are most alike? Answers will vary.

2. Which pair names things that are most unlike? ______

C. On the lines after the words below, write the names of two other items that are similar to each object named. Possible answers:

1. pencil ball-point pen crayon
2. pan pot cup
3. flute trombone clarinet
4. shirt coat sweater
5. hat cap scarf
6. cup mug pan

Name ______

Teacher Note
Discuss pupils' responses to part B. Encourage pupils to support their opinions with reasons. Then have pupils share their answers to part C.

Identifying Structure

The word **structure** refers to how something is built. A poem can be written by following a certain structure. Haiku is a type of Japanese poem that tells about something in nature and brings a certain feeling or mood to the reader. Haiku has its own special structure. For example, each line has a set number of syllables. Read the two examples of Haiku and then answer the questions about their structure.

Gently falling flakes
Blanketing the winter ground
Soft and wet and white.

Beating on the roof
Lightning flashing in the sky
Trees bent in the wind.

1. How many lines does each poem have? __3__
2. How many syllables are in the first line? __5__
3. How many syllables are in the second line? __7__
4. How many syllables are in the third line? __5__
5. Does Haiku have to rhyme? __no__

Name ____________________

Teacher Note
Help pupils understand that the structure of Haiku refers to the number of lines, the number of syllables per line, and the absence of rhyme. Discuss the mood or kind of feeling created by each poem. Then have groups of pupils work together to write their own Haiku.

Identifying Structure

The structure of a story is the plan that is used to construct the story. Most stories follow a similar plan. It includes a setting, characters, and a plot. The **setting** tells the time and place of the story. The **characters** are the people or animals that the story is about. The **plot** is the sequence of events from the beginning, to the high point in the action, to a satisfactory ending.

From the list at the right, choose and write a plan for a story. Choose a time, place, and characters. Then write a sentence to show how you will begin, another to show the most exciting part of the action, and a third to tell how you will end the story. You may prefer to think of your own story parts. Answers will vary.

long ago
last year
across the sea
on a ranch
deep in the forest
a girl on crutches
an adventurous boy
a wild pony
no one knew what happened
late one night
just as the hero
what a big splash
you can still see the spot
maybe some other time

Time ______________________ Place ______________________

Characters ____

Beginning ____

____

High Point ____

____

Ending ____

____

Name ____

Teacher Note
Review the various story elements with the class. Encourage pupils to use their own elements if the ones on the page do not appeal to them. Have pupils share their finished work. Ask the rest of the class to identify the story elements—time, place, characters, and so on—in each presentation.

Steps in a Process

A **process** is the order in which something is done. Read the process described below. Then rewrite the sentences so that the steps are in the correct order.

Making a Bird Feeder

Punch four small holes in the plastic tray, one in each corner. Tie the four string ends together so your feeder will hang. Collect the materials you will need: a plastic tray from a supermarket package, 4 pieces of string about 20 inches long, peanut butter, cereal. Spread peanut butter on the bird-feeder tray. Knot each string at one end, and draw the other end through one of the holes in the tray. Sprinkle cereal, such as oatmeal, on the peanut butter. Hang your feeder and watch the birds enjoy it!

1. Collect the materials you will need: a plastic tray from a supermarket package, 4 pieces of string about 20 inches long, peanut butter, cereal.
2. Punch four small holes in the plastic tray, one in each corner.
3. Knot each string at one end, and draw the other end through one of the holes in the tray.
4. Tie the four string ends together so your feeder will hang.
5. Spread peanut butter on the bird-feeder tray.
6. Sprinkle cereal, such as oatmeal, on the peanut butter.
7. Hang your feeder and watch the birds enjoy it!

Name ______________________

Teacher Note
Caution pupils to read the material carefully before attempting to order it. When pupils have finished, discuss why the order makes a difference. For instance, what would happen if the peanut butter were put on too soon? Pupils might enjoy following up on this page and making the bird feeder according to their reordered directions.

Steps in a Process

A. Number the boxes to show the order in which the squares were shaded. Put **1** under the first box and continue with **2, 3, 4, 5, 6, 7,** and **8**.

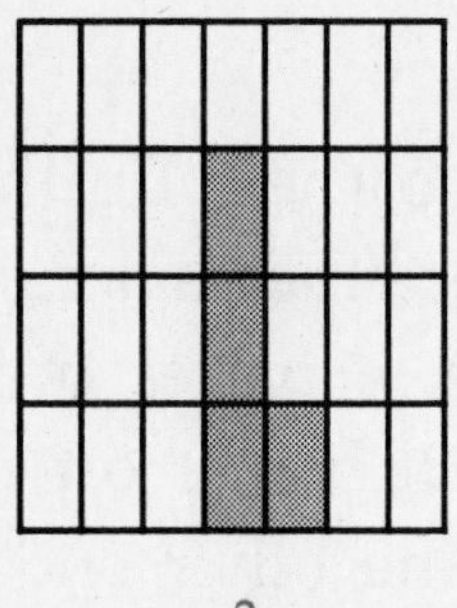

3

6

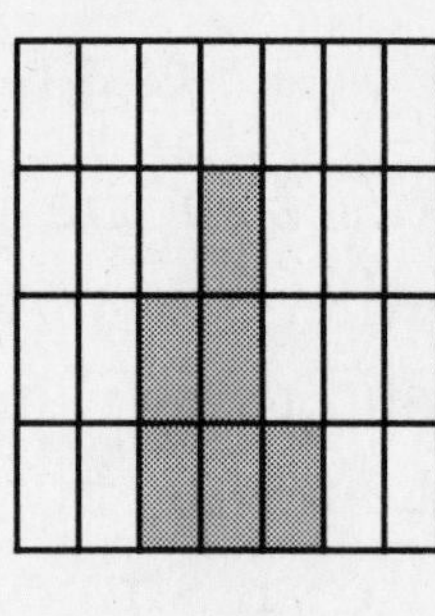

4

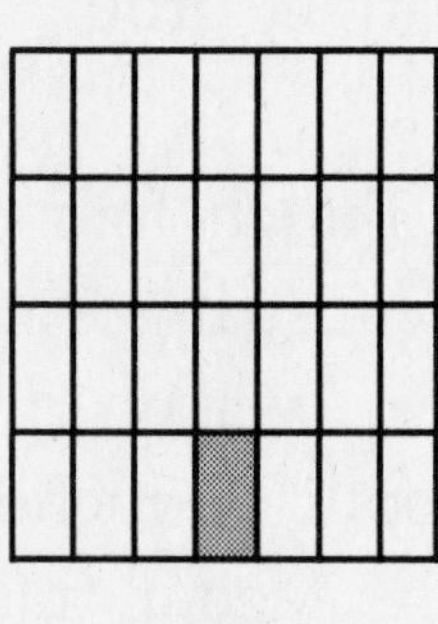

1

8

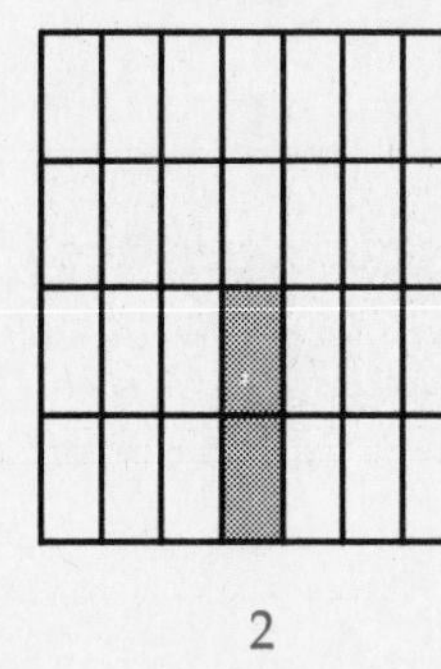

2

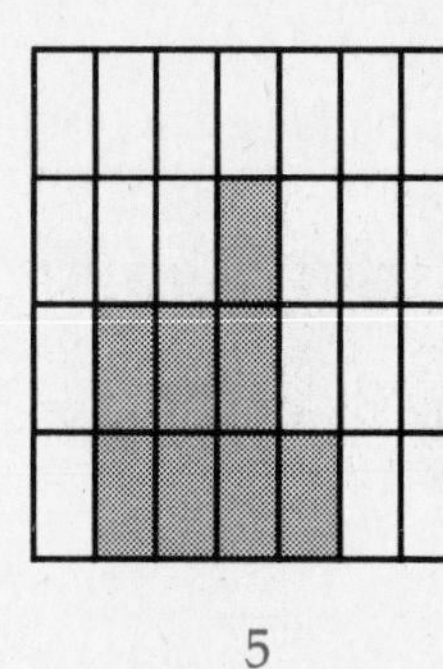

5

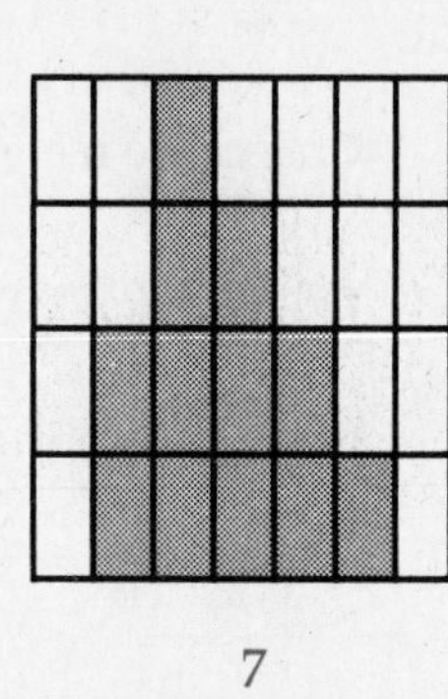

7

B. Tell the order in which you will make something. It may be an art project, some food, or whatever you choose. Write the title of your project on the first line. Then list six steps. Write the steps in order.

Responses will vary.

1. __________
2. __________
3. __________
4. __________
5. __________
6. __________

Name __________

Teacher Note
After pupils finish part A, ask them to explain why the squares had to be shaded in this order. Have pupils share their responses to part B. Other pupils might check the sequence by attempting to follow the directions their classmates wrote.

SKILL 9

Figural Relationships

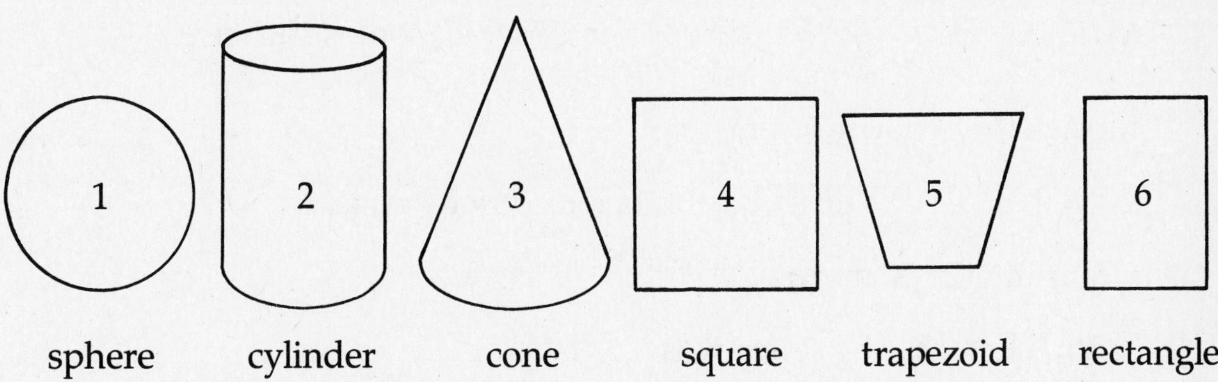

When you study geometric shapes, you learn how to describe the world in mathematical language. In this drawing of part of an airport, you can find many geometrical shapes. Label each geometrical shape in the picture, using the numbers of the shapes shown above. Answers may vary.

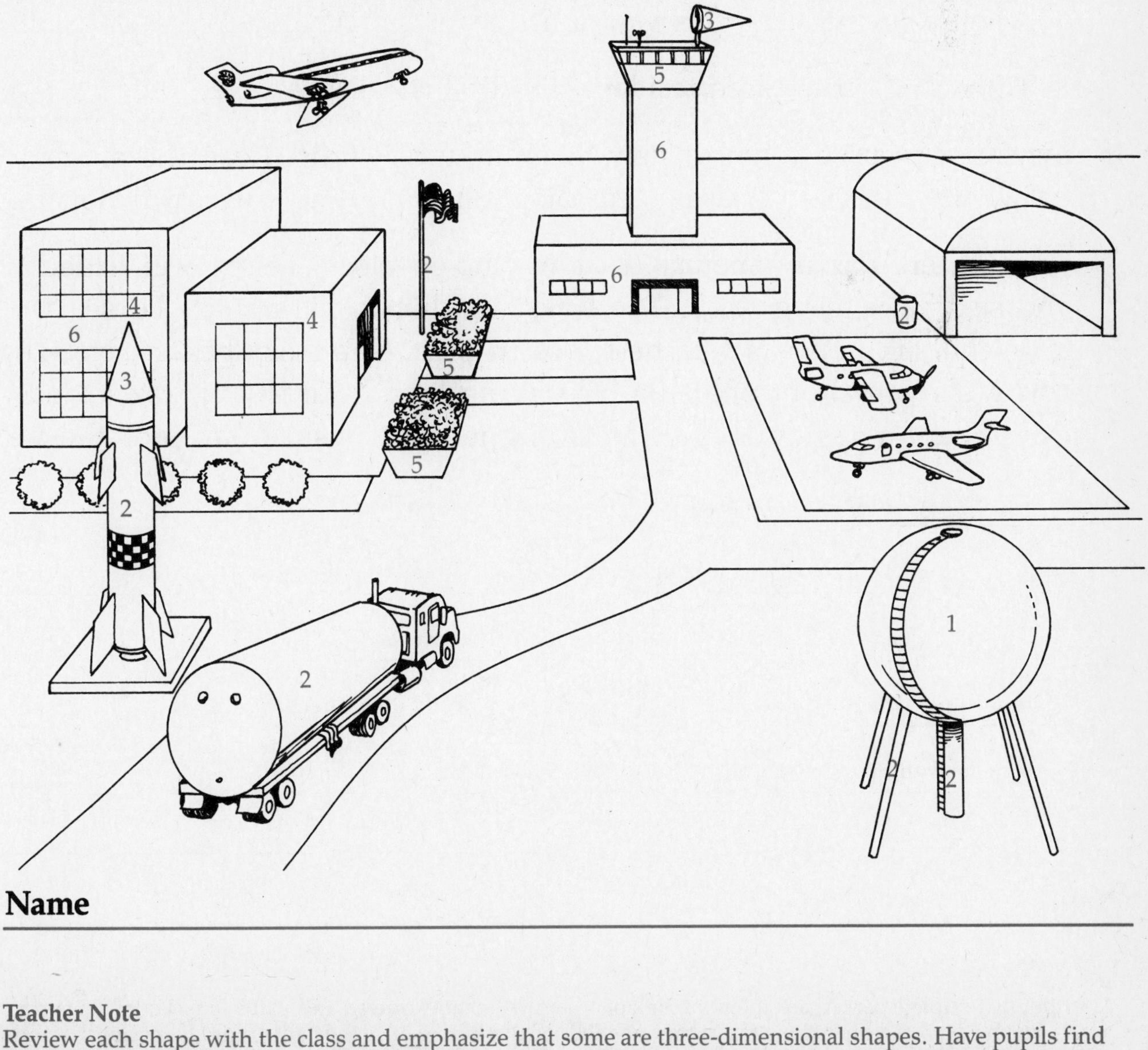

Name ______________________________

Teacher Note
Review each shape with the class and emphasize that some are three-dimensional shapes. Have pupils find examples of each shape within the classroom.

Figural Relationships

A **figure** can be a symbol or representation of something else.

A. Complete the following sentences.

The symbol **X** is used for a number of different things.

1. In arithmetic, **X** means to multiply.
2. In **W**, **X**, **Y**, **Z**, the letter **X** is part of the alphabet.
3. We could say, "**X** out the part that you do not want."
   This would mean to mark out something.

Another symbol used for many things is a line: —.

4. When a line is used this way, **ā**, it means long a.
5. When you write **vice-president**, the line is called a hyphen.

B. Symbols are used to show how to pronounce words. Read the article below. Then rewrite it using regular spelling. You may use a dictionary.

In t̶h̶ə érli daz in əmerəkə, t̶h̶âr wér nō envəlōps. Letərz wér fōlded and sēld wit̶h̶ sēling waks. T̶h̶ə waks wəz bôt in härd stiks. Tü sēl ə letər, t̶h̶ə stik ov waks wəz held klōs tü ə fīr. T̶h̶ə waks bēkām soft. T̶h̶ə soft waks wəz dropt ontü t̶h̶ə bak ov t̶h̶ə letər hwâr t̶h̶ə ej wəz fōlded ōvər. T̶h̶en, ə pēs ov metəl wit̶h̶ ə pikcher wəz pusht doun intü t̶h̶ə waks.

In the early days in America, there were no envelopes. Letters were folded and sealed with sealing wax. The wax was bought in hard sticks. To seal a letter, the stick of wax was held close to a fire. The wax became soft. The soft wax was dropped onto the back of the letter where the edge was folded over. Then, a piece of metal with a picture was pushed down into the wax.

Name ______________________

Teacher Note
After pupils complete part A, ask them to think of other ways that *X* is used and that a line is used. When pupils finish part B, ask them how much they needed the dictionary once they got going. Point out that most symbols are easily read.

SKILL 10 Comparing Word Meanings

Homographs are words that are spelled alike but are not pronounced alike. Their meanings are also different.

In the pairs of sentences below, find the homographs and circle them. Put a check before each sentence in which the circled word has a long vowel sound. Then write a definition for each circled word that has a check before it.

__√__ 1. Marge had a (tear) in the corner of her eye.

_____ Please do not (tear) the page in that book.

drop of water from the eye

_____ 2. The bird-watcher saw a beautiful (dove.)

__√__ Janice (dove) into the deep water.

go in head first

__√__ 3. Lester will (read) his report to the class.

_____ Ruth has (read) five library books this week.

look through and understand meaning

_____ 4. How long did your grandparents (live) in that town?

__√__ Is that a dead wasp or a (live) one?

alive or living

__√__ 5. You must (wind) the clock if you want it to work.

_____ There is a strong (wind) blowing toward us.

turn

Name ____________________

Teacher Note
After pupils complete the page, check on comprehension by having volunteers read aloud each sentence. Have the class give definitions for the words that did not have a long vowel sound. You might also ask pupils to think of additional homographs and write sentences using them.

Comparing Word Meanings

Each word in the box is the opposite, or **antonym**, of an underlined word in the sentences below. Write each word from the box on the line beside the sentence that contains its antonym.

tame	many	rough	straight	love	shout	push
lower	usually	quiet	leave	correct	foolish	false

1. rough Mr. King polished the stone until it was shiny and smooth.
2. shout Whisper when you tell me the secret.
3. many Few students are in the library now.
4. usually Jennifer rarely rides the bus to school.
5. correct Sam didn't want to give the wrong answer.
6. tame Lions and tigers are wild animals.
7. straight The scouts followed the crooked path through the woods.
8. push Pull the handle to open the drawer.
9. false Roger told me an unusual but true story.
10. lower José asked Larry to raise the window shade.
11. quiet It's noisy in the school yard during recess.
12. foolish Sarah was wise to take her friend's advice.
13. leave No one may enter the building until nine o'clock.
14. love Don't you hate to stay inside on a rainy day?

Name ____________________

Teacher Note
As pupils give other examples of antonyms, write them on the chalkboard. Then have pupils write one sentence for each pair of antonyms.

Identifying Main Ideas

A. Choose the main idea for the story from the box. Write the sentence on the first line of the story.

> Early bicycles did not have pedals.
> Early bicycles were made almost entirely of wood.
> Early bicycles were hard to ride.

Early bicycles were made almost entirely of wood.

The wheels were wooden. A wooden crossbar held the wheels together. Another wooden crossbar steered these bicycles. Some wooden bicycles were so rough to ride, they were called "boneshakers."

B. One test of a main-idea sentence is to see if the other sentences help to explain or develop it. Underline the sentence in each group below that best expresses the main idea of the group.

1. a. Wild turkeys live in small flocks in the woods.
   b. Turkeys build their nests on the forest ground.
   c. At night wild turkeys rest in trees.
   d. For food they eat wild nuts, berries, seeds, and insects.

2. a. Trace the design on a large bar of soap.
   b. Use a knife to cut the soap.
   c. Rub the soap lightly to take off any rough edges.
   d. Interesting figures can be carved from soap.

3. a. If danger is near, the mother springs away in big hops.
   b. Mother kangaroos protect their babies in many ways.
   c. Since young kangaroos are smaller than mice when they are born, they must stay in their mother's pouch for several months.
   d. Since mother kangaroos can run thirty miles per hour, they can outrun most of the animals that might harm their babies.

Name ______________________________

Teacher Note
After the class has completed part A, discuss why the answer given is better than the others. Have pupils complete part B, and review their answers. If pupils err in their choices, point out how all the other sentences would not relate to the incorrect sentence.

Identifying Main Ideas

The **main idea** of a paragraph may be found in the first or last sentence, or even in the middle of the paragraph. Underline the main-idea sentence in each paragraph below.

1. Many accidents happen on sidewalks. People may fall over toys which have been left in the way. Muddy or icy spots may cause one to slip and fall. Holes in the cement also cause people to fall.

2. The alligator dozes on the bank of the stream, appearing to be asleep. Suddenly it lashes out with its tail to kill some creature who is nearby. The alligator is sly when it comes to catching food.

3. Although they are fascinating today, old-time trains were really quite uncomfortable to the passengers of long ago. The seats were rough and bumpy. The cars were open to wind, rain, and sun.

4. Paper is made from wood. Medicine is made from bark. A tree is a very useful plant. Its leaves provide shade and beauty. Its roots soak up water which might have washed away soil.

Name ____________________

Teacher Note
After pupils complete the page, discuss the answers. Help pupils note how the other sentences in the paragraphs help support or tell more about the main idea.

Identifying Main Ideas

If a main idea is repeated in a slightly different way, its meaning will often become clear. In each paragraph below, underline the sentence that gives the main idea. Then put a check by the sentence you would choose to be the paragraph's closing sentence. The closing sentence should repeat the main idea stated in the sentence you underlined.

1. The sea horse is a fish that isn't anything like a fish. It has a head like a horse and a tail that curls like a monkey's. It carries its young in a pouch like a kangaroo. It has bumps on its skin and can change color to hide from its enemies.

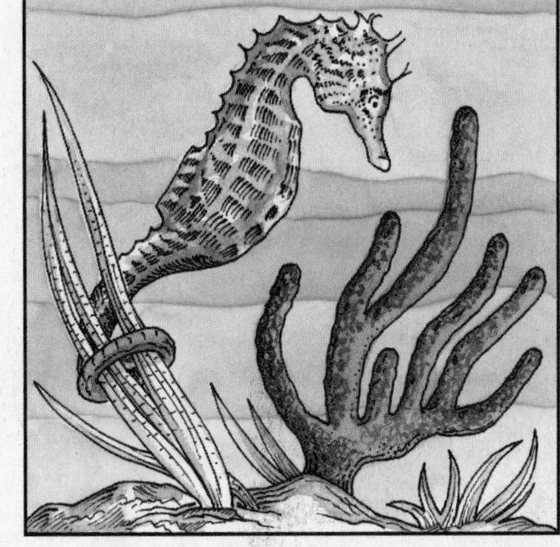

✔ The sea horse is not your usual fish.

_____ The sea horse got its name because it looks like a horse.

2. The roadrunner is a flightless bird that has rattlesnakes for dinner. It kills the rattlesnake by kicking and pecking it. How does this bird manage to avoid the rattlesnake's deadly bite? The roadrunner moves very quickly. It can run as fast as 20 miles (32.2 km) per hour and jump as high as 10 feet (3m). So, when the rattlesnake tries to strike back with its fangs, the roadrunner can usually get out of the way in time.

_____ The most dangerous snake in the desert is the rattlesnake.

✔ This small bird is one of the rattlesnake's worst enemies.

Name ______________________________

Teacher Note
Help pupils understand that the last sentence of a paragraph often restates the main idea. Ask pupils to think of other sentences that restate the main idea of each paragraph.

Identifying Main Ideas

A. Study the picture. Then choose the main idea from the box and underline it.

People enjoy waiting in line at the bank.
People expect to wait in long lines at the bank.
People get upset if they have to wait in long lines at the bank.

B. Write five details from the picture that support the main idea you chose. Answers will vary.

1. woman pointing at teller
2. woman's arms in air
3. child crying
4. man looking at watch
5. man's hands on hips

Name ______________________

Teacher Note
Have pupils complete the page and then share their answers with the class. Make sure that all the details mentioned support the main idea. Ask pupils to name other ways that people show annoyance that were not portrayed in the picture.

Identifying Relationships

One thing often causes another thing to happen. This is called a **causal** (cause/effect) **relationship**.

A. Some causes and effects are listed below. Put the letter of the effect on the line before the most likely cause.

	Causes	Effects
g	1. Hiking in the woods alone	a. supplies new scientific facts about the universe.
e	2. Being polite	b. keeps germs from spreading.
h	3. Cheering at a football game	c. sometimes saves you money.
f	4. An oil spill	d. helps you learn to work well with others.
b	5. Staying clean	e. makes other people happy.
j	6. Swimming	f. may kill sea life.
a	7. Sending astronauts into space	g. might cause you to get lost.
d	8. Playing on a team	h. may make your voice hoarse.
i	9. Digging many wells	i. may lower the level of water.
c	10. Growing your own vegetables	j. helps develop muscles.

B. Put **X** on the line before each sentence that shows a cause and effect relationship.

X 1. I tripped on the rug and hurt my knee.

X 2. Reading books often helps increase your knowledge.

____ 3. We probably won't go tomorrow.

____ 4. The snowstorm lasted most of the night.

Name

Teacher Note
Before pupils begin the page, have them give examples of cause and effect relationships. After the page is completed, discuss the answers with the class. Point out that although playing on a team (item 8) may have the effect of developing muscles (j), the more likely result is helping you learn to work well with others (d). Ask pupils to think of possible effects that sentences 3 and 4 in part B could have.

Identifying Relationships

A. Place a check before the three sentences below that contain a cause-effect relationship. Circle the part in each sentence that contains the cause.

___√___ 1. (Rain fell all day Saturday,) so we could not play outside.

___√___ 2. (Because the grass was becoming yellow,) Mrs. Smith watered her yard yesterday.

___√___ 3. (Since it is so sunny and warm,) we will go on a picnic.

______ 4. Sixteen people left Sunday, but only fifteen people returned on Monday.

______ 5. Tonight is cool and rainy, although last night was rather warm.

B. Complete each sentence by writing an effect that could result from the cause given. Answers will vary.

1. Because of the violent storm, ______________________________

______________________________.

2. Jason was late for the party so ______________________________

______________________________.

3. After Deke had a big lunch, ______________________________

______________________________.

4. Since today is a holiday, ______________________________

______________________________.

5. Ling spilled popcorn on the floor ______________________________

______________________________.

Name ______________________________

Teacher Note
Remind pupils that although a sentence may have two clauses, the clauses need not have a causal relationship. Discuss why sentences 4 and 5 do not show cause-effect. Have pupils share their answers to part B and discuss any that do not show a causal relationship.

Identifying Relationships

Events can be related by time. Events can happen at the same time, or before or after one another.

A. Put a check before the sentences in which one event happens before another. Put **X** before sentences that describe events that happen at the same time.

X 1. As I was leaving, the paper was delivered.

✓ 2. My birthday is May 30, and school is out June 16.

X 3. The bus arrived just as we came outside.

X 4. While my class studies English, Judy's class works on math.

X 5. Mr. Lee does his cleaning when it rains.

B. Complete the following sentences with an event that happens after the one given. Answers will vary.

1. Our science projects are due in January. ______________________

2. Steve looked at the calendar. ______________________

3. Amy goes to the store. ______________________

4. David had to search for his roller skates. ______________________

Name ______________________

Teacher Note
After pupils complete the page, go over the sentences in part A and discuss the words that are clues to the kind of time relationship shown. Have pupils share their answers to part B and note the words they used to show sequential time (for example, *then*, *next*).

Identifying Relationships

Some things are related because of their position in space.

Study the map. Then answer the questions or follow the directions.

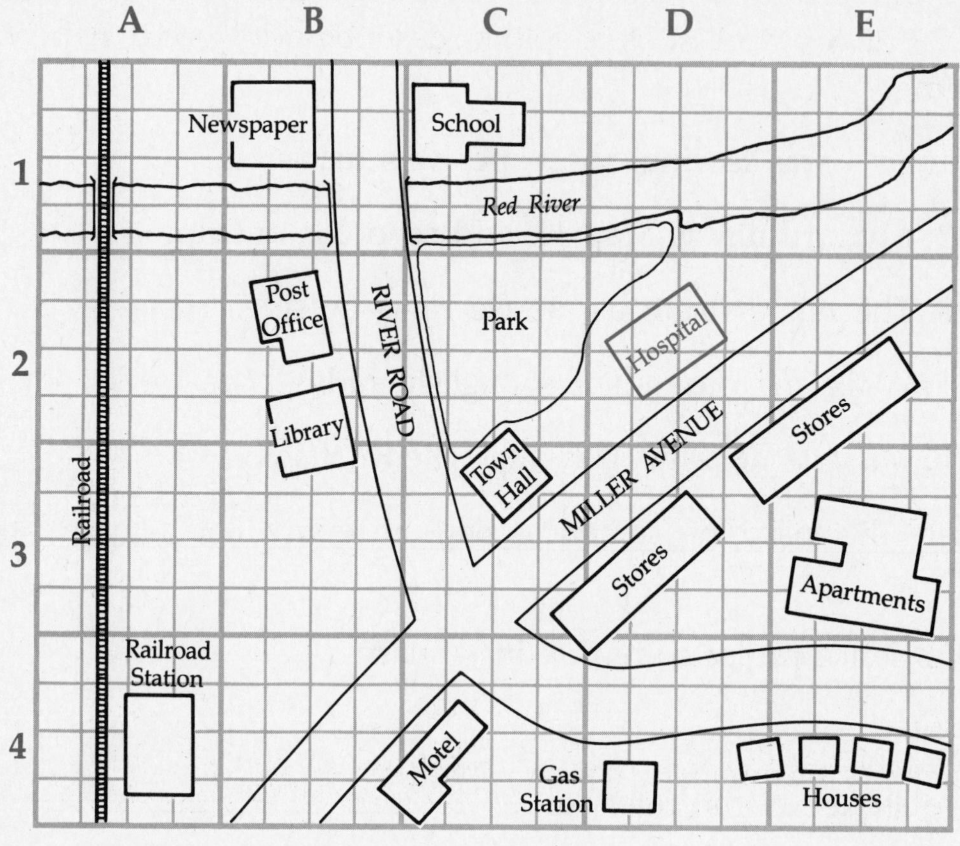

1. In what square would you find the school? C1
2. If Mr. Valdez lives in square E3, what kind of home does he live in?

   apartment
3. Anita Wang works in the building next to the library. Where does she work? post office
4. The community is planning to build a hospital next to the town hall. In what square will that be? D2 Draw and label the hospital on the map.

Name ______________________

Teacher Note
Explain that the map has a grid on it to make it easier to locate places. Tell pupils to name the grid squares by giving the letter first and then the number; for example, A1 is the first square at the top left. After pupils have completed the page, ask them where they feel a good location for a restaurant would be. Be sure they give reasons for their choices.

A. Comparing and Contrasting

Shapes may be alike even though they are turned around. Study each shape on the left. Then circle the shapes on the right that are the same as the one on the left.

1. 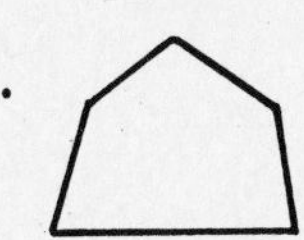

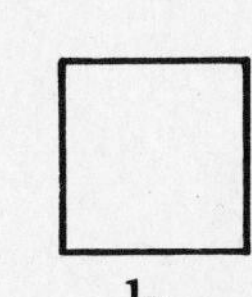

a. b. c.

2. 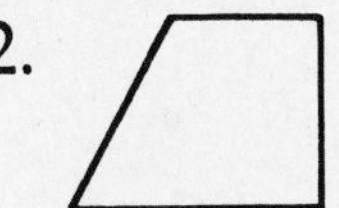

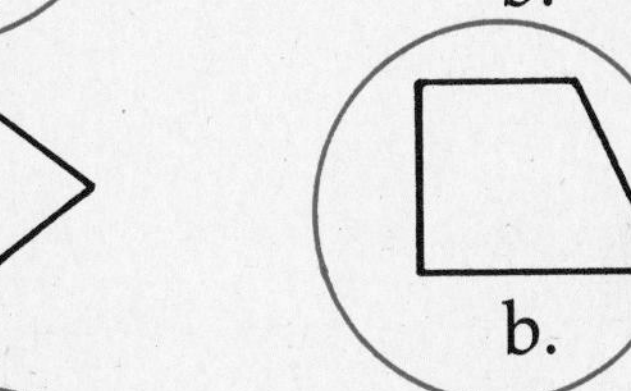

a. b. c.

3. 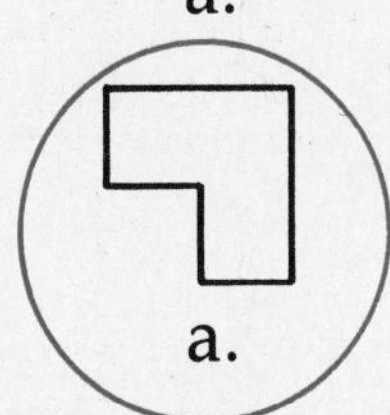

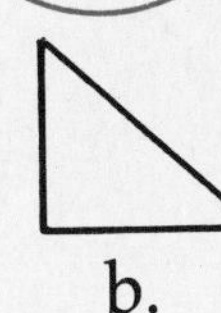

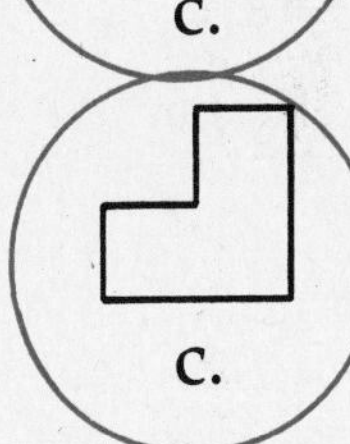

a. b. c.

B. Identifying Relationships

Three shapes in each group are related to one another. Find the shape that is different and put **X** on it.

1. 

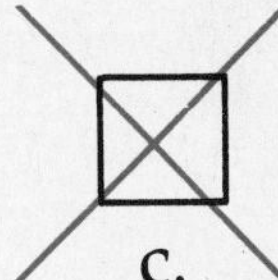

a. b. c. d.

2. 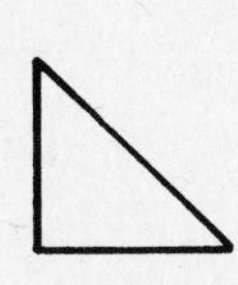

a. b. c. d.

3. 

a. b. c. d.

Name ______________________

Teacher Note
After completing the page, pupils may discuss and check their work with you or a partner.

C. Identifying Structure

A **synonym** is a word that means just about the same thing as another word. To form the pairs of synonyms below, take a letter from the top word and use it to make a new word from the bottom word. Write the synonyms on the lines.

Example: tint **tin**
meal **metal**

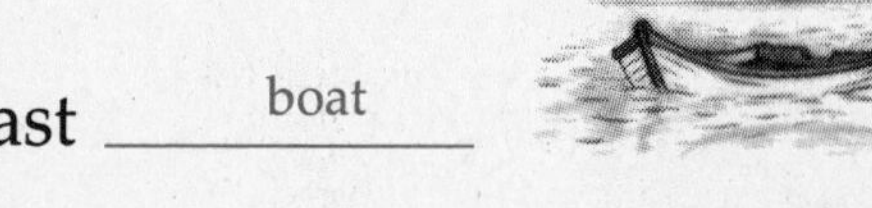

1. boast ___boat___
hip ___ship___

2. brush ___bush___
tee ___tree___

3. stalk ___talk___
peak ___speak___

4. trip ___rip___
ear ___tear___

D. Comparing Word Meanings

Change the meaning of each word by adding one of the prefixes in the box.

super	semi	re

1. ___re___ call
2. ___re___ make
3. ___semi___ private
4. ___super___ sonic
5. ___re___ port
6. ___super___ natural
7. ___re___ do
8. ___semi___ circle
9. ___re___ read

Name ________________________________

Teacher Note
After completing the page, pupils may discuss and check their work with you or a partner.

UNIT 3

Applying

Teacher Note
In order to develop Bloom's third stage—applying—the pupil needs to engage in the following skills:
- Ordering Objects
- Estimating
- Anticipating Probabilities
- Inferring
- Interpreting Changes in Word Meanings

Applying means using what you know. Look at the picture. Where do you think the two girls are? Why is each girl wearing a number? Does the picture show what event they will take part in? Do the girls look like they are enjoying themselves? What do you think they might do next?

Ordering Objects

Arrange each list in order according to the directions above it. Write **1, 2, 3, 4,** or **5** on the line before the word. **A** has been started for you.

A. from little to big

1 bee
4 child
3 cat
2 bird
5 whale

B. from fast to slow

4 rabbit
2 airplane
5 turtle
3 car
1 spacecraft

C. from high to low

2 house
4 dog
5 insect
1 skyscraper
3 refrigerator

D. from old to young

5 baby
4 toddler
3 first grader
1 grandparent
2 teenager

E. from hot to cold

3 rain
1 fire
4 ice water
2 warm soup
5 ice

F. from easy to difficult

Answers will vary.

____ landing a plane
____ giving a speech
____ painting a picture
____ riding a bike
____ driving a bus

Name ______________________________

Teacher Note
After pupils complete the page, discuss their answers for item F. Point out that what we perceive as easy or difficult has a lot to do with our knowledge. For example, if you don't know how to ride a bicycle, that task would seem more difficult than something you know how to do.

Ordering Objects

Arrange the items in each group below according to size or amount, from smallest to largest. Write the items in order.

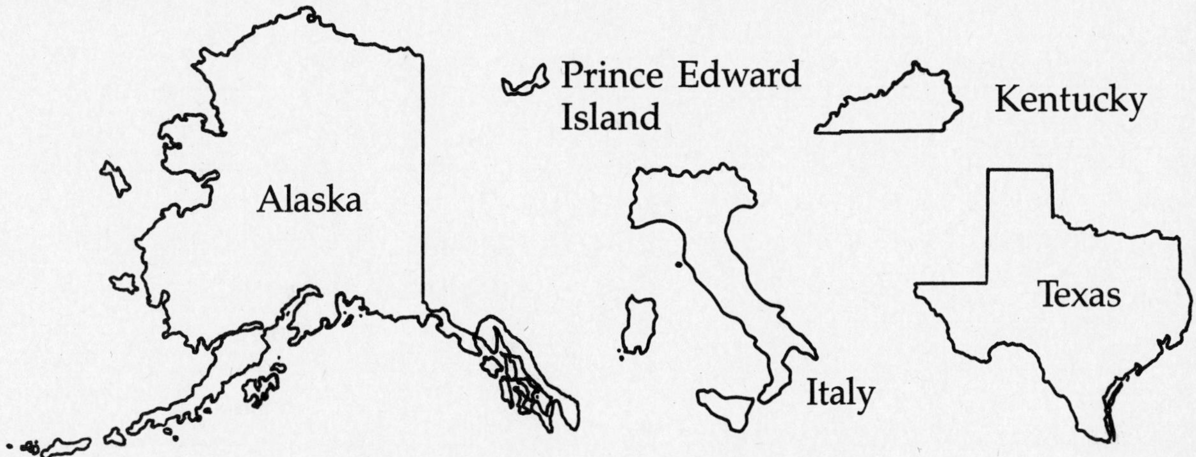

1. Alaska, Prince Edward Island, Italy, Kentucky, Texas

   Prince Edward Island, Kentucky, Italy, Texas, Alaska

2. 145, 115, 1045, 105, 150, 11054

   105, 115, 145, 150, 1045, 11054

3. one-tenth, one-fourth, one-half, one-third, one-fifth

   1/10, 1/5, 1/4, 1/3, 1/2

4. marble, basketball, golf ball, baseball, beach ball

   marble, golf ball, baseball, basketball, beach ball

5. baby, teenager, adult, child

   baby, child, teenager, adult

6. day, second, week, hour, weekend

   second, hour, day, weekend, week

7. decade, year, century, month

   month, year, decade, century

8. car, rollerskate, motorcycle, bicycle

   rollerskate, bicycle, motorcycle, car

Name ______________________

Teacher Note
Have pupils complete the page independently. If they are unsure of any words, have them use a dictionary. Follow up the page by having pupils make their own lists of related items and asking classmates to order them according to size.

Ordering Objects

There are many kinds of **order**. You can put the same things in different orders for different purposes.

Use the words in the box in each exercise below.

stool	horse	human	snake	mosquito

A. List the items by height, from shortest to tallest.

1. mosquito
2. snake
3. stool
4. human
5. horse

B. Arrange the items according to alphabetical order.

1. horse
2. human
3. mosquito
4. snake
5. stool

C. Arrange the items according to the number of legs each one has, from the smallest number to the largest.

1. snake
2. human
3. stool
4. horse
5. mosquito

D. Arrange the items according to how much they eat, from the least to the most.

1. stool
2. mosquito
3. snake
4. human
5. horse

Name ______________________________

Teacher Note
Before pupils begin, point out that in parts C and D there may be items that have no legs or do not eat at all. Tell pupils that these items should be listed first in each category. When the class has completed the page, encourage pupils to think of additional ways of ordering the items.

Estimating

When you **estimate**, you make a guess that is based upon what you see or what you already know. In Parts A and B, you will use what you can see or what you already know to help you estimate.

A. The giraffe in the middle is ten feet (three meters) tall. Estimate the height of the giraffe on the left, the height of the giraffe on the right, and the height of the tree.

Height of: Estimates may vary.

1. Giraffe at left 8 ft. or about 2.5 m
2. Giraffe at right 12 ft. or about 3.5 m
3. Tree 15 ft. or about 4.5 m

B. Look at the map. It took Kevin 40 minutes to ride his bike from Glidden to Silver City. Estimate how long it will take him to ride from:

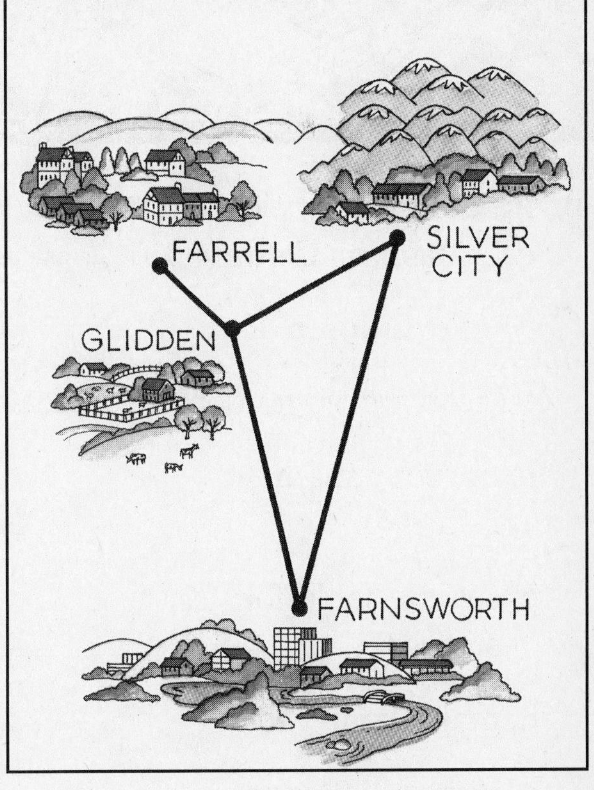

Estimates may vary.

1. Glidden to Farnsworth

   60 minutes / 1 hour

2. Glidden to Farrell

   20 minutes

3. Farnsworth to Silver City

   80 minutes / 1 hour 20 minutes

Name ______________________

Teacher Note
Help pupils understand that an estimate is not exact. Upon completing the activities, allow pupils to use rulers or other means of measurement to see how accurate their estimates were. Discuss other factors that might influence the times given in Part B.

Estimating

A. Estimate in your head the price of each item in **Column 2**. Then circle the item or items that you could buy with the amount of money listed in **Column 1**. Estimates will vary.

Column 1	Column 2
a. $ 5.00	pen, pad of paper, crayons, greeting card, picture frame
b. $ 10.00	record, tape, radio, watch, television
c. $ 25.00	gloves, earmuffs, coat, ski cap, boots
d. $ 50.00	pillow, bedspread, blanket, sheet, towel
e. $100.00	wagon, rocking horse, doll, electric train set, book

B. In **Column 2** below, write how long you think it would take you to do each task in **Column 1**. Estimates will vary.

Column 1	Column 2
a. clean up your room	______
b. do your math homework	______
c. set the table for supper	______
d. make your bed	______
e. write a letter to a friend	______

Name ______

Teacher Note
Pupils' answers will vary according to their experience and knowledge. You might bring in catalogs or newspaper clippings advertising some of the items mentioned so that pupils can measure their estimates against them. For part B, have pupils time themselves at the activities listed to check their estimates. Discuss the value of making good estimates when shopping or doing tasks.

Anticipating Probabilities

Some things are very likely to happen. These are called **probabilities.** Other things are unlikely to happen. They are not probabilities.

Read each statement. If it tells about something that is very likely to happen, write **probability** on the line before it.

probability 1. Summer will be warmer than fall.

probability 2. Miss Thomas, who is an actress, will have a lot to say about our play.

probability 3. Mr. White will pay his bill next Friday because there is a penalty for paying after that date.

_______ 4. Melissa saw many black clouds in the sky on a sunny day.

probability 5. Sarah has a broken leg and won't run in the race today.

probability 6. You will celebrate your birthday sometime this year.

_______ 7. We will go swimming in the Arctic Ocean.

_______ 8. If your team plays ball against a team of high school students, your team will win.

probability 9. If you exercise more than your friend, you will be stronger.

probability 10. If you draw and paint well, you have talent in art.

Name _______________________

Teacher Note
After pupils complete the page, discuss the answers. Then ask pupils why they were able to pick out the probabilities. Help them see that probabilities are things that usually happen a certain way. In other words, probabilities are based on experience. Discuss why it is useful to be able to anticipate probabilities.

Anticipating Probabilities

For each situation below, there are three different endings. Put **1** before the ending that is **most likely** to happen. Put **2** before the ending that could **possibly** happen. Put **3** before the ending that is **not very likely** to happen.

A. Rick is the smallest player on the basketball team. He practices often and is determined to be a good player. Rick will probably be

__3__ the worst player on the team. Answers may vary.

__1__ about as good as the other players.

__2__ one of the better players.

B. George has just moved to the city and does not know his way around the neighborhood. Late one afternoon, while walking down a street, he becomes so interested in the sights that he forgets to watch where he is going. He will probably

__2__ feel lost and ask a police officer to take him home. Answers may vary.

__1__ wander around until he finds a familiar street.

__3__ walk all evening until his family finally finds him.

C. It has always been difficult for Jane to write stories. She wants to improve, so she probably will

__2__ ask a friend to help her. Answers will vary.

__1__ ask for help from her teachers at school.

__3__ work with a professional writer from the newspaper.

Name ______________________________

Teacher Note
Explain that there are often several probabilities to a given situation and that some are more likely than others. Have pupils complete the page; then discuss their answers. Point out that probabilities are not certainties and that they are all possibilities.

Anticipating Probabilities

Using the information shown in the pictures, decide which explorer will probably get out of the cave first. On the lines below the pictures, explain your decision.

Picture 1

Picture 2

Answers may vary, but most students will pick the man in picture 2 because he has better light, a walkie-talkie to get help, and doesn't have any problems such as broken glasses.

Name

Teacher Note
When pupils complete the page, discuss the pictures and their answers. Point out that to choose picture 1 you would have to rely more on imagination, ingenuity, and hope than on the probabilities. You might also want to point out that in certain situations it is these characteristics that enable people to overcome the actual probabilities.

Anticipating Probabilities

Read the story. Then follow the directions below it.

The story of Rip Van Winkle takes place in the 1700's in the Catskill Mountains of New York. Rip was a farmer, but as his wife was always telling him, he was not a very good one.

One day Rip went out hunting in the woods. There he met a man dressed in old-fashioned clothing who was carrying a keg. Rip helped the man carry the keg up a mountain. At the top they met other men dressed like the first one. Rip and the men had a feast and then Rip fell asleep.

When Rip woke up, twenty years had passed. During this time Rip's wife had died and his children had grown up. Many other changes had taken place in Rip's village and in the country itself. The colonists had won the Revolutionary War and the United States was now an independent nation.

Imagine that you had an experience like Rip Van Winkle's and fell asleep for twenty years. What changes would probably take place during that time? Why do you think so?

Answers will vary.

Name

Teacher Note
Explain that the story of Rip Van Winkle is a condensation of a famous story by Washington Irving. In Irving's version, when Rip wakes up, he learns that the men he met were from Henry Hudson's ship which had been in America long before Rip's time. Have pupils share their answers and discuss the validity of the probabilities they predict.

Inferring

To **infer** means to look at the evidence and come to a conclusion based on that evidence. That is, you look at the facts, and you **infer** the answer.

A. The sentences below give facts about objects. Infer what each object is, and write its name on the line.

ruler
1. It is long and narrow. It measures things. You may keep it in your desk.

rain hat, boot, swimsuit
2. You wear it outdoors. It does not cover a very large area of your body. You don't mind if it gets wet.

pencil, crayon, chalk
3. This is long and narrow, but it gets shorter each time you use it.

fireworks
4. These objects glow and sparkle in the dark. We often see them in many colors on the Fourth of July.

lunch
5. You often carry this in a paper bag to school. You enjoy it at noon or when you go on a picnic.

toothbrush
6. This long stick has short bristles on one end. We are supposed to use it after meals and before we go to bed.

B. On the lines below, describe an object without naming it. Give facts that will enable a reader to infer what the object is.

Answers will vary.

Name

Teacher Note
When pupils complete the page, go over the answers with the class. Accept any reasonable alternatives that pupils suggest. Have them take turns challenging one another with the descriptions they wrote.

Inferring

Each group of pictures shows a silly race. The tracks made by the winner are also shown. Study the racers and the tracks carefully. Then write the winner on the finish line.

1.

The winner: chimney sweep

2.

The winner: girl with wheelbarrow

3.

The winner: boy on pogo stick

Name ______________________

Teacher Note
Point out to pupils that they must study the pictures carefully before answering the questions. Discuss the answers with the class. Ask pupils to explain how they made their inferences. Then challenge pupils to make their own pictures in which the winner of a race can be identified only by his or her tracks.

SKILL 16 Inferring

Read each story and the sentences that tell about each person. Underline the sentence that tells who spoke.

1. The team is playing the last baseball game of the season. This is the last inning and the score is tied. The two players have struck out and now the bases are loaded. Someone says, "I'm sure I can help the team win with a base hit. I'll probably even hit a homer."

   a. Gus, who does not brag, is one of the team's better hitters.

   b. Lee has made many hits this year and is very sure of herself.

   c. Joe, the pitcher, has had one hit so far this year.

2. Last Thursday, Mr. Grant asked if someone would stay after school to help him clean the chalkboards. One student offered, "I will, Mr. Grant. You can count on me."

   a. Linda's brother was coming home today after spending two years in the navy.

   b. Rita's mother was going to the dentist and expected Rita to watch her younger brother after school.

   c. Lenny's parents both work until six o'clock and won't be home.

3. Terry didn't know that her friends were planning a surprise birthday party for her. She wondered why everyone stopped talking when she came by or why they giggled so much. She was also puzzled when someone said, "Terry, this will be a weekend you'll never forget."

   a. Ivan likes to brag.

   b. Jim has trouble keeping a secret.

   c. Cindy is jealous of Terry.

Name ______________________________

Teacher Note
When pupils complete the page, go over their answers. Ask pupils to point out the words or phrases in the stories that led them to their inferences.

Inferring

A. Read the sentences. Write your inferences on the lines following them.

1. Wei has finished giving her oral book report, and she is smiling. The other students are clapping. Wei has done a good job.

2. Sam keeps his boots in his locker. He has just come in from recess with wet feet. Sam left his boots in his locker when he went outside for recess.

3. Sandy's lunch is gone, and her books are missing. Sandy stopped to play on the way to school. Sandy left her lunch and books where she stopped to play.

B. Sometimes you can draw different inferences from the same set of facts. Write your own inferences for these statements.

1. Nell stops to examine a wound on her leg. She is wearing roller skates. A large dog is running down the street. Possible: Nell fell while roller skating. The dog bit Nell.

2. Eric is holding several packages from his favorite store. He is walking slowly with his neighbor, Mr. Grand, who has just recovered from an operation. Possible: Eric is carrying Mr. Grand's packages. Eric met Mr. Grand on his way home from the store and is carrying his own packages.

Name ______

Teacher Note
Discuss pupils' inferences in part A. Accept any logical variations. Before pupils begin part B, tell them to write at least two inferences for each situation. Have pupils compare their inferences. Discuss which are the most reasonable and why.

Changes in Word Meanings

In a **figure of speech** each word does not mean what it usually does. Instead, the words together have another meaning.

Read each sentence with a figure of speech. Then write what the sentence really means on the lines.

1. Earl was up to his neck in work.

   Earl had much work to do.

2. Ann wasn't dressed well today, but you shouldn't judge a book by its cover.

   Do not judge Ann by the way she is dressed.

3. My parents explained, "You must take care of your dog. You can't have your cake and eat it, too."

   You must be responsible for your dog if you want to keep it.

4. It seemed as if Jeff had broken the wagon, but we may have been barking up the wrong tree.

   Jeff probably was wrongly accused.

5. Robin jumped out of her skin when I dropped that book.

   Robin was scared.

6. We thought the comedian at the party was just a barrel of laughs.

   We thought the comedian was very funny.

7. When the boys broke the window, they decided to face the music and tell the owner.

   The boys decided to face the consequences.

8. Their lives hung by a thread as they battled the storm at sea.

   Their lives were in great danger.

Name ______________________________

Teacher Note
Give examples of figures of speech before pupils begin the page (*seeing stars, butterflies in my stomach,* and so on). Encourage pupils to think of others. Have the class complete the page and then discuss the answers. Pupils might enjoy illustrating literally one or more of the figures of speech on the page.

SKILL 17

Changes in Word Meanings

A **prefix** is a group of letters added to the beginning of a word to change its meaning. The prefixes **un-**, **im-**, and **in-** are prefixes that change the meaning of a word to the opposite of its original meaning.

A. Add the prefix **un-**, **im-**, or **in-** to each of the words in the box. Write the new word and its meaning. Use a dictionary if you are not sure of a word.

Example: passable-impassable

possible	accurate	fashionable	polite	clear

1. impossible — not capable of being done
2. inaccurate — not correct
3. unfashionable — out of style
4. impolite — rude
5. unclear — fuzzy, hazy, not clear

B. Write each word below **without** its prefix. Then give its new meaning.

1. unsafe safe — secure
2. immature mature — adultlike
3. immobile mobile — able to move
4. inconsiderate considerate — thoughtful

Name ______________________

Teacher Note
Have pupils use dictionaries to complete the page. After the page is finished, ask pupils to use some of these words in sentences of their own. Have the class name other words whose meaning can be changed by the prefixes *un-*, *in-*, or *im-*.

A. Ordering Objects Inferring

Read the paragraph and study the pictures. Then number the pictures **1** to **5** to show the correct order.

Shane lives at 122 Brick Lane. On his way to school he sees Mrs. Jaye's dog and then Mr. Gray's cat. Before long, Shane sees the school.

Name ______________________

Teacher Note
After completing the page, pupils may discuss and check their work with you or a partner.

B. Changes in Word Meanings
Estimating

Each of the pictures on this page represents a word with the word **can** in it. Write each word and its meaning below the picture that represents it. You may want to check a dictionary. Before you begin, estimate how long you think it will take you to complete this page. Write your estimate on the line. Then time yourself to see how close you were.

Estimated time: ______________ Real time: ______________

1. 

candle-stick of wax that has a wick and is lit for light

2. canoe - light, thin boat

3. 

canary - yellow songbird

4. 

canopy - tentlike roof held up by posts

5. 

cancel - to give up; mark used

6. 

canister - a metal container

Name ______________________________

Teacher Note
After completing the page, pupils may discuss and check their work with you or a partner.

UNIT 4

Analyzing

Teacher Note

In order to develop Bloom's fourth stage—analyzing—the pupil needs to engage in the following skills:

- Judging Completeness
- Judging Relevance of Information
- Distinguishing Abstract from Concrete
- Judging Logic of Actions
- Organizing Elements of a Selection
- Examining Story Logic
- Recognizing Fallacies

Analyzing means seeing how parts fit together. Tell what is happening in the picture. What is the person doing? How do you know? Why is the person looking through the machine? Would the person see as clear a scene without the machine? Can you tell what the person is trying to see?

SKILL 18 Judging Completeness

There are many problems that can be solved only if you have all the necessary information, or **complete** information.

In each word problem below, some information is missing. Read the problem. On the line after it, write the information you would need before you could solve the problem.

1. Rosemary has 170 sheets of paper which she wants to divide among her classmates. How many sheets will each student get? how many students are in the class

2. Howard has sixteen postcards. David has fifteen, and Lee has more than either Howard or David. How many postcards do the boys have altogether? how many postcards Lee has

3. Theresa and Jenny have some stickers. Theresa has more than Jenny. The girls want to divide the stickers equally. How many stickers will each one get? how many stickers each girl has

4. Paul plans to buy a yo-yo for $1.50, some colored pens for $3.00, and some postage stamps. How much money will he need? how much the stamps cost

5. Tammy travels 17 miles on the school bus each day. Gordon travels even more miles on his trip to and from school. How many more miles does Gordon travel than Tammy? how many miles Gordon travels

Name ______________________

Teacher Note
Read the introduction aloud with the class to be sure everyone understands the directions. Have pupils complete the page on their own. Then discuss why each piece of information is necessary to solve the problem. Ask pupils to think of other examples where complete information would be needed to solve a problem.

Judging Completeness

In a report, a writer should give exact and complete information.

A. Read the report below. Find and underline three sentences in the report that need more information.

Most people think that sand deserts are the only kind of desert. That is not true. Some deserts are covered in other ways besides sand. However, all deserts are alike in one way.

Desert plants and animals need little water. Some plants, such as the cactus, are well-suited for dry desert climates. The reason for this is interesting.

B. Use an encyclopedia or other reference book to find more exact information for the sentences you underlined in part A. Then rewrite the report, using the facts you have found to make the sentences more complete.

Answers will vary.

Name ____________________

Teacher Note
You may wish to check pupils' answers to part A before pupils go on to part B. When they have rewritten the report, ask volunteers to share their work. Discuss the various ways pupils chose to make the report more complete and informative. Make the point that this is a useful lesson to remember when pupils work on reports of their own.

Judging Completeness

Sometimes you can fill in the facts to a story to make it complete by careful observation.

A. Study the picture carefully. Then answer the questions.

Answers may vary.

1. What is happening in the picture?

hurricane or big storm — tree has fallen; man cannot get by

2. Explain why you think so.

wind is blowing trees, sky is dark, tree has blown down, man is out of car, a woman is coming to help — umbrella inside-out

B. Suppose the house in the picture is yours, and you want to call the highway department in your town to tell them about the fallen tree. Write the complete information the people at the highway department will need to know so that the tree can be removed.

your name, address, phone number, street the tree is down on

C. Complete the paragraph about the picture in your own words. Answers may vary.

The hurricane was very fierce, destructive. The rain and wind caused a lot of damage. Most people stayed home, but Dr. Brandon was out in his car making a housecall. However a fallen tree kept him from getting through. Mrs. Newman, who lived in the house nearby, came out to see if she could help.

Name ______________________

Teacher Note
Have pupils complete part A. Then discuss their answers. (Details that pupils submit may vary.) Have pupils complete parts B and C independently. Compare pupil responses, stressing completeness in part B. Pupil responses in part C may vary somewhat.

Relevance of Information

Relevant information is information that is important to you.

Put a check by the two sentences that tell the most important things to do in order to successfully complete each activity. Answers may vary.

1. Buy a bicycle

_____ Check the kind of tires the bicycle has.

__√__ Compare the quality of different kinds of bicycles.

_____ Decide which color looks best.

__√__ Visit some stores to compare prices.

2. Try out for beginners' band

_____ Tell the band teacher all about yourself.

_____ Let the band teacher know that your parents are musical.

__√__ Follow directions carefully during the tryout.

__√__ Be quiet unless you are asked to talk or play an instrument.

3. Make a project for the science fair

__√__ Begin early so you will have enough time to work on it.

_____ Make a fancy project which uses only costly materials.

__√__ Find a project you're interested in and can do by yourself.

_____ Help plan the science fair.

4. Race in the school track meet

__√__ Practice every day for several weeks before the track meet.

_____ Enter every event that you can.

_____ Help your coach by being nearby when you might be needed.

__√__ Do the best you can.

Name ________________________________

Teacher Note
Remind pupils to check the two most important things, even though some of the others are also possible actions. When pupils finish the page, discuss their responses. Ask pupils to explain why the other choices are not as relevant as the ones they selected.

Relevance of Information

Some scientists plan a trip to Antarctica and decide to take their families along. Suppose that your family is part of the group. Which five facts below will be most relevant to a family preparing for a stay in Antarctica? Put **R** before the five facts that seem most relevant to you.

Answers may vary.

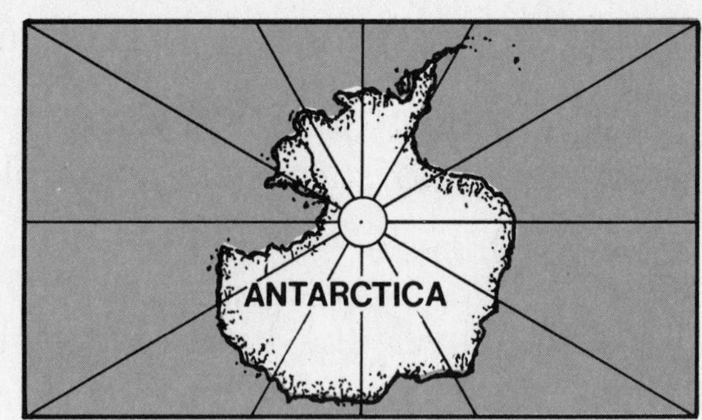

R 1. Heavy clothing is worn all year long at the South Pole.

____ 2. Antarctica is a vast, frozen wasteland.

R 3. It is difficult to get supplies during some months of the year.

____ 4. There are no highways in Antarctica.

R 5. The wind can be very destructive in polar areas.

R 6. You will spend a lot of time indoors in Antarctica.

____ 7. Modern technology has helped to make cold areas more livable.

____ 8. Seals, fish, whales, and penguins live along the Antarctic seacoast.

____ 9. Antarctica is larger than Australia.

R 10. Frostbite can occur even when you are careful about protecting your skin.

Name ____________________

Teacher Note
Review the concept of relevancy with the class before assigning this page. After pupils have completed it, go over their answers. Discuss why some facts would be more helpful than others in this situation. Ask pupils to defend each fact they checked by telling why they think it would be important to know that and how it would affect them in preparing for the trip. Accept all reasonable and logical explanations.

Abstract or Concrete

Some words are more general than others. For instance, the word **woman** is more general than the word **Judy**, because **woman** refers to a whole group of people and **Judy** refers to one person. When words are general, we say they are **abstract**. When words are specific, we say they are **concrete**.

A. Circle the more concrete word in each pair below. The first one is done for you.

1. gem, (diamond)	2. room, (kitchen)	3. clothes, (suit)
4. boy, (Carl)	5. food, (steak)	6. (robin,) bird
7. (cat,) animal	8. flower, (rose)	9. (maple,) tree

B. Number the words **1**, **2**, or **3** according to how concrete or abstract they are in relation to one another. The most concrete word in each group should be numbered **1**. The most abstract word should be numbered **3**.

1. __3__ person	__2__ boy	__1__ Jesse
2. __1__ rose	__3__ plant	__2__ flower
3. __2__ cereal	__3__ food	__1__ oatmeal
4. __3__ vehicle	__1__ jeep	__2__ car
5. __1__ shoe	__2__ footwear	__3__ clothing
6. __3__ water	__1__ Atlantic	__2__ ocean

Name ______________________________

Teacher Note
Go over the introduction and illustration with the class before assigning the page. Be sure pupils understand that *abstract* means general here and that *concrete* means specific. Have the class complete parts A and B and then discuss their answers.

Abstract or Concrete

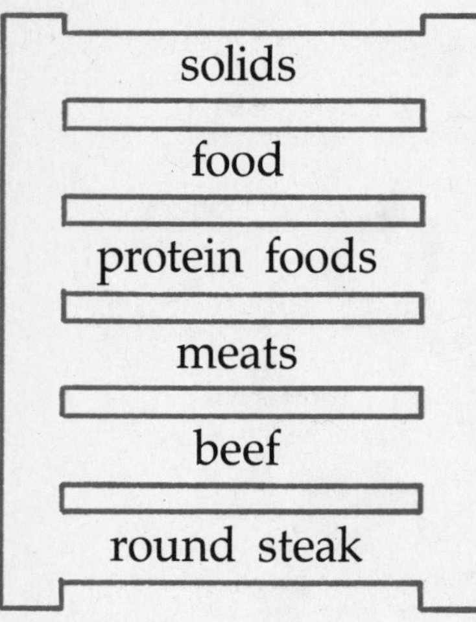

A very specific name of an item is on the bottom step of the ladder. As you climb the steps, you find names of broader groups or categories. On the top step is the broadest category into which all the other names belong.

Read the three lists of names below. Put each group in order by writing the names on the numbered ladders. Put the most specific name at the bottom, and the broadest name at the top.

1. sweaters, outerwear, blue sweaters, clothes
2. birds, green parakeets, parrot family, parakeets, Tweetie (your parakeet)
3. house, shelter, buildings, split-level house, homes

1.

clothes

outerwear

sweaters

blue sweaters

2.

birds

parrot family

parakeets

green parakeets

Tweetie (your parakeet)

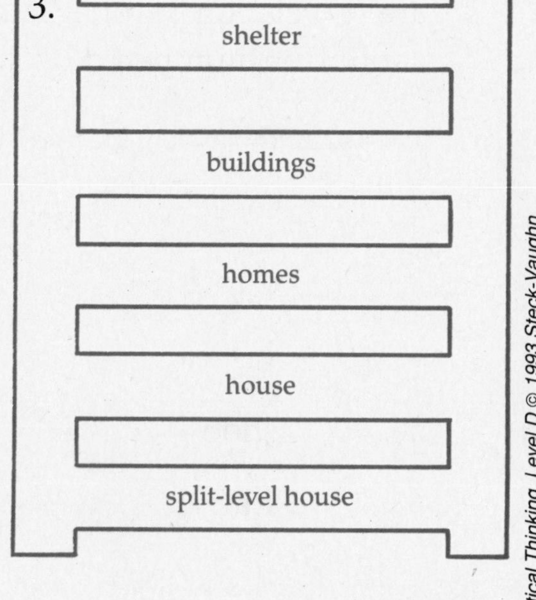

Name ______________________________

Teacher Note
Discuss the introduction to the page and the example. Explain that round steak is a kind of beef, beef is a kind of meat, and so on. Point out that the most abstract name will go at the top of each ladder and the most specific or concrete name will go at the bottom. Have pupils complete the page. Then discuss their responses.

SKILL 21 Logic of Actions

Read each problem or task. Then choose an item from the box that will help solve the problem or do the job. Write your choice on the line.

hammer	recipe	needle	saw	dime
pull toy	vase	bookmark	thermometer	rake
ice	rope	trash bin	toaster	ruler

needle 1. You want to remove a splinter from your finger.

recipe 2. You need to know how much cinnamon to put in a fruit dessert.

trash bin 3. You want to throw away some litter.

rope 4. You need to tie down the flaps of a heavy box.

bookmark 5. You want to mark a place in a story that you are reading.

pull toy 6. You want a present for a one-year-old child.

toaster 7. You want to brown some bread for breakfast.

vase 8. You want to arrange some flowers for the table.

saw 9. You want to cut some logs for a fire.

rake 10. You want to clean up the leaves in your yard.

Name ______________________________

Teacher Note
Explain that *logic* means making the most sense. When pupils have completed the page, discuss their answers. Ask pupils to suggest what the five remaining words in the box—*ice, dime, ruler, thermometer,* and *hammer*—would be useful for.

SKILL 21 — Logic of Actions

Read each statement. Put a check by the course of action that best completes each sentence.

1. Amy wanted to meet the new girl sitting on the steps across the street. When she saw her, Amy ______.

   ________ watched her for a while

   ___✔___ went over and introduced herself

   ________ went back into her house

2. Sabrina wanted to be good enough to play on the softball team, so she ______.

   ___✔___ practiced her hitting

   ________ never went to any games

   ________ met the team members

3. Mom's birthday was only a week away. Brian needed money to buy her a birthday present, so he ______.

   ___✔___ mowed his neighbor's lawn to earn money

   ________ waited until he could save enough of his allowance

   ________ told Mom he didn't have enough money

Name ________________________________

Teacher Note
Help pupils understand that using logic means doing what makes sense. Have pupils explain the logic of their choices. Have the class discuss other logical courses of action for the situations described above.

Read the story below. Then answer the questions about it.

Cindy and Carla were nine-year-old twins who lived on a ranch. On the first Saturday of May, they brought their twin calves to the county fair. The girls groomed the little animals and then waited for the calf-judging contest to begin.

At last the contest was announced. The two girls, dressed alike in jeans and checked shirts, came out with their look-alike calves. The people in the stands thought they were seeing double!

Cindy and Carla won the top prize easily because the sight of the two sets of twins was so striking.

1. Who are the two main characters? Cindy and Carla

2. Where and when does the story take place? at the county fair on the first Saturday in May

3. What happens **first**, **next**, and **last** in the story? The girls take their calves to the fair, groom them, and take part in the contest.

4. How does the story end? The girls win the top prize.

Name __________

Teacher Note
Explain to pupils that one way to analyze a story is to look at the various elements that make it up. After pupils have completed the page, ask them to suggest a good title for the story.

Elements of a Selection

Read each story below.

I was born in a nest tucked away in a large barn. I have eleven brothers and sisters who were also born the same day I was. My brothers and sisters and I are white, and we have small pink eyes. (It was several days after we were born that we could open our eyes, however.) We also have long tails and fine whiskers. Now that we are a little older, we are beginning to explore our home. I think a barn is a dandy place for a little mouse to live!

Mr. Calvin decided to go for a ride in his new jeep. He invited Mac to go along with him. The two of them climbed into the jeep and set out for town. Mr. Calvin waved to friends and neighbors as they went by. People waved and called out, "Hi, Mac! Hi, Mr. Calvin!" Everyone admired the new jeep. At the Goode Foode Shoppe, Mr. Calvin got out and bought some yogurt for himself and for Mac. They sat on the curb and ate it. "You know, Mr. Calvin," said the man who owned the Goode Foode Shoppe, "I think it's nice that you treat your dog just like a person."

A. Write a title for each story.

1. Answers will vary. ____________________

2. ____________________

B. Tell who the narrator, or voice, in each story is. Is it someone named in the story, or is it an outside narrator who sees the action but does not take part in it?

1. a little mouse ____________________

2. an outside narrator ____________________

Name ____________________

Teacher Note
Explain that a narrator can be first person (I) or third person (someone else who sees the action of the story but does not take part in it). Have pupils complete the page. Then discuss the various titles suggested by the class. Review the story elements from page 77 and have pupils name the main characters and describe the setting, plot, and ending for each of these stories.

Story Logic

Study the pictures below. Number them **1** to **4** so that they are in a logical order. Then, under each picture, write a sentence or two to tell what is happening.

4

The boy used the ladder to rescue

the kitten in the tree.

2

The boy answered the phone

and looked out the window.

1

The phone rang while the boy

was studying.

3

The boy got a ladder.

Name ______________________

Teacher Note
Have pupils complete the page. Then check to see if their stories are logical. Review the elements of a story from pages 77-78 by asking pupils to make up a title and to name characters, setting, plot, and ending for the story.

Story Logic

If a sentence is **logical**, it makes sense. It fits correctly with the information that comes before it.

Read each group of sentences below. If the last sentence is logical, put a check before the number.

> **Example:** Parrots can learn to talk. Greenie is a parrot. Greenie can learn to talk. (The last sentence is logical because it fits correctly with the information before it. It makes sense.)

___√___ 1. All of my friends like to swim. Bobby is my friend. Bobby likes to swim.

______ 2. Many animals have brown-and-white coloring. Candy has a beautiful dog. Candy's dog is brown and white.

___√___ 3. Anita does not like to be around wasps. Arnold has wasps by his house. Anita doesn't like to go to Arnold's house.

___√___ 4. Most plants are green. The holly fern is a plant. The holly fern is probably green.

______ 5. Tom does not like school very much. Elsie does like school. Tom and Elsie don't like each other.

______ 6. Many people have brown hair and brown eyes. George is a person. George has brown hair and brown eyes.

______ 7. Some students in this school are female. The other students are male. There are more females than males in this school.

___√___ 8. Kathy is always on time. Kathy is coming to my house. Kathy will be punctual unless something unexpected happens.

Name ______________________________

Teacher Note
Discuss the example. Ask pupils to explain why the third sentence is a logical conclusion based on the information provided in the first two sentences. When pupils complete the page, ask them to explain why each final sentence is logical or not.

Recognizing Fallacies

An **analogy** is a special kind of comparison.

In each analogy below, decide how the first two words are related. Then relate the second two words in the same way by choosing a word from the word box.

alphabet	climb	king
mountain	light	foot
bottom	dig	soup
island	find	pool

1. **clean** is to **dirty** as **top** is to bottom
2. **run** is to **track** as **swim** is to pool
3. **creek** is to **river** as **hill** is to mountain
4. **finger** is to **hand** as **toe** is to foot
5. **feel** is to **touch** as **discover** is to find
6. **drum** is to **band** as **letter** is to alphabet
7. **bang** is to **noise** as **flash** is to light
8. **girl** is to **boy** as **queen** is to king
9. **broom** is to **sweep** as **shovel** is to dig
10. **stove** is to **cook** as **ladder** is to climb
11. **frame** is to **picture** as **water** is to island
12. **glass** is to **milk** as **bowl** is to soup

Name ______________________

Teacher Note
Explain that a *fallacy* is something that is erroneous or wrong. Then discuss analogies. Complete the first analogy together. Point out that the words *clean* and *dirty* are opposites, so the next pair of words must be related in the same way. Have pupils select the word from the box that is the opposite of *top*. When pupils finish the page, ask them to explain how each pair of words is related.

SKILL 24

Recognizing Fallacies

In some analogies the second pair of words is not related in the way that the first pair is. Such analogies are called **false analogies**. Look at the example below.

> **Example: night** is to **moonlight** as **day** is to **school**
> The first two words, **night** and **moonlight**, show the relationship that the last two words must have in order for the analogy to be true. But the words **day** and **school** do not have the same relationship that the words **night** and **moonlight** have, so the analogy is false. In order for the analogy to be true, the last term must be **sunlight**.

A. Read each analogy below. Underline each false analogy.

1. **person** is to **house** as **bird** is to **nest**
2. **book** is to **read** as **pencil** is to **measure**
3. **hand** is to **glove** as **foot** is to **sock**
4. **ice cream** is to **cold** as **hot chocolate** is to **breakfast**
5. **mother** is to **father** as **aunt** is to **nephew**

B. The last word of each analogy below is missing. Write the word that will complete the analogy correctly.

1. **sun** is to **day** as **moon** is to night
2. **water** is to **liquid** as **ice** is to solid
3. **spaghetti** is to **eat** as **coat** is to wear
4. **light** is to **dark** as **below** is to above
5. **chair** is to **sit** as **bed** is to sleep
6. **field** is to **football** as **court** is to tennis/basketball
7. **book** is to **read** as **television** is to watch
8. **sidewalk** is to **pedestrians** as **street** is to vehicles (cars, etc.)

Name ______________________

Teacher Note
Go over the introduction to the page with the class. Discuss the concept of false analogies. Point out that these are fallacies because they are not true. Have pupils identify the false analogies in part A and supply the correct word to complete each analogy in part B. Discuss pupils' responses. Allow for any reasonable variations from those given.

Recognizing Fallacies

A. Some "either-or" statements are true because, at times, only two choices are possible. But some "either-or" statements are false because there could be more than two choices to consider. Write **true** or **false** before each "either-or" statement below. The first one is done for you.

false 1. Water is either hot or cold.

false 2. A house pet is either a dog or a fish.

false 3. A president is either young or old.

true 4. The lights are either off or on.

false 5. Your hair is either blonde or brown.

false 6. Either you like to work or you don't like to work.

true 7. The store is either open or closed.

false 8. Winter weather is either snowy or rainy.

B. For each false statement above, write the number of the statement and list some other choices which should have been included. The first one is done for you.

1. warm, cool, boiling, lukewarm

2. cat, gerbil, mouse, rabbit, turtle

3. middle-aged

5. black, gray, white, red

6. like it a little or sometimes

8. sunny, cloudy, foggy, warm, breezy, cold

Name ______________________

Teacher Note
Mention that some *either-or* statements are fallacious because they limit a situation to two choices when many more might be possible. Have pupils complete the page and then share their answers to part B.

Recognizing Fallacies

A **loaded word** is one that plays on your emotions in order to persuade you to think, do, or buy something.

A. Read the advertisements below and circle the loaded words.

Example: Bonny Wipes are a real (bargain) for (clever) shoppers. Try these (new) and (improved) tissues. Answers may vary.

1. I was (ashamed) of my (embarrassing) dandruff until I used Flakeoff.
2. My (new) Dirtyrinse does a (fantastic) job on clothes.
3. Gobble removes the (toughest) stains (faster) and (easier.)
4. A (smart) shopper like you can't (afford) to miss this (special) sale.
5. Seethrough is (softer) and (more absorbent than other) towels.
6. This is your (last chance) to (save) money on a Hotstuff Water Heater.
7. The year's (best value) is this Safari Flashlight.
8. Bones Plus gives your dog (special nutrition) and (extra calcium.)

B. Use the lines below to write an ad for pet skunks. Use loaded words to try to persuade your readers that skunks make terrific pets!

Answers will vary.

Name

Teacher Note
Discuss the definition of a *loaded word*. Then go over the example. When pupils complete the page ask them to explain why they circled specific words. Answers may vary slightly, but pupils should demonstrate an understanding of a loaded word. Have pupils share their skunk ads. Ask the class to decide which ads are the most persuasive. Have them explain why.

A. Judging Completeness

All the things pictured below were returned to the store because they were incomplete. Under each item write what is missing.

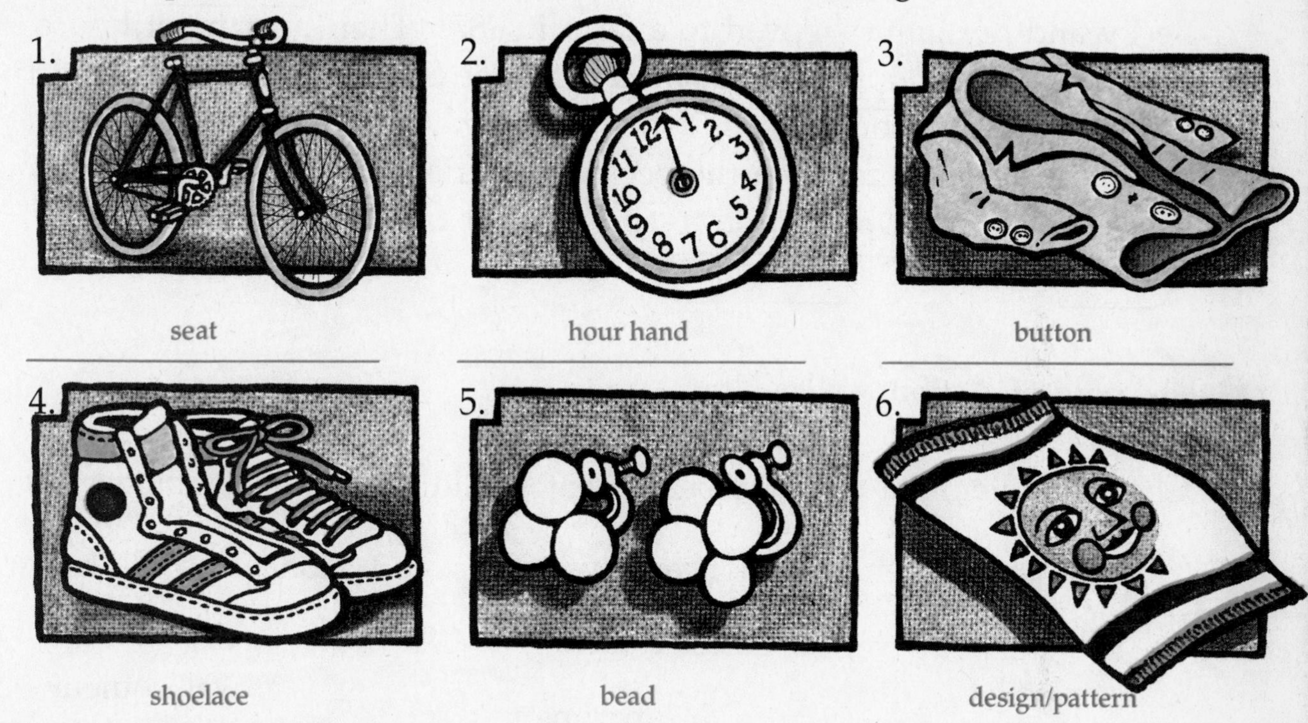

B. Abstract or Concrete

Notice the dark words in each sentence below. Put **1** above the word that is most concrete. Continue numbering the words up to **4** so that the most abstract word is numbered **4**.

1. Mrs. Norton wanted some **accessories** [4] for her new outfit, so she stopped at the **jewelry** [3] counter to look at **earrings** [2] and selected a pair of **drop earrings** [1].
2. Helen took her **coat** [2] back to the **clothing** [4] store because a **slicker** [1] was not the kind of **outdoor gear** [3] she wanted.

Name ________________________________

Teacher Note
After completing the page, pupils may discuss and check their work with you or a partner.

C. Story Logic

Read the story below and circle the words that are not logical.

Becky and her family moved to a farm in 1870. Their (apartment) house was near a large (shopping mall.) Becky's father cleared the land around the house and planted some crops. When Becky wasn't helping out on the farm, she went swimming in the (ocean) with friends or rode around town on her (skateboard.) On Saturdays, she and her family sometimes went to the (movies) in their (station wagon.)

D. Logic of Actions

Check the items in each list below that would be logical for pioneers to do.

1. Pioneers made their own
   - ✓ clothes
   - ✓ candles
   - ___ home movies
   - ✓ brooms

2. Pioneers lived in
   - ___ trailers
   - ___ apartments
   - ✓ log cabins
   - ✓ sod houses

3. Pioneer scouts learned to
   - ✓ walk quietly
   - ___ use snowmobiles
   - ✓ track animals
   - ___ use walkie-talkies

4. For fun, pioneers
   - ___ watched TV
   - ✓ square danced
   - ✓ told stories
   - ✓ sang songs

Name ______________________

Teacher Note
After completing the page, pupils may discuss and check their work with you or a partner.

UNIT 5

Synthesizing

Teacher Note

In order to develop Bloom's fifth stage—synthesizing—the pupil needs to engage in the following skills:

- Communicating Ideas
- Planning Projects
- Building Hypotheses
- Drawing Conclusions
- Proposing Alternatives

Synthesizing means putting information together to come up with new ideas. Look at the picture. What are the girls doing? Can they understand each other? How do you know? Is one learning from the other? Why or why not? What are some other ways people communicate?

SKILL 25 Communicating Ideas

A **rebus** is a kind of puzzle in which pictures are used in place of words or parts of words. The rebus below uses pictures for syllables.

A. Draw a picture for each missing syllable in the rebuses below. The first is done for you.

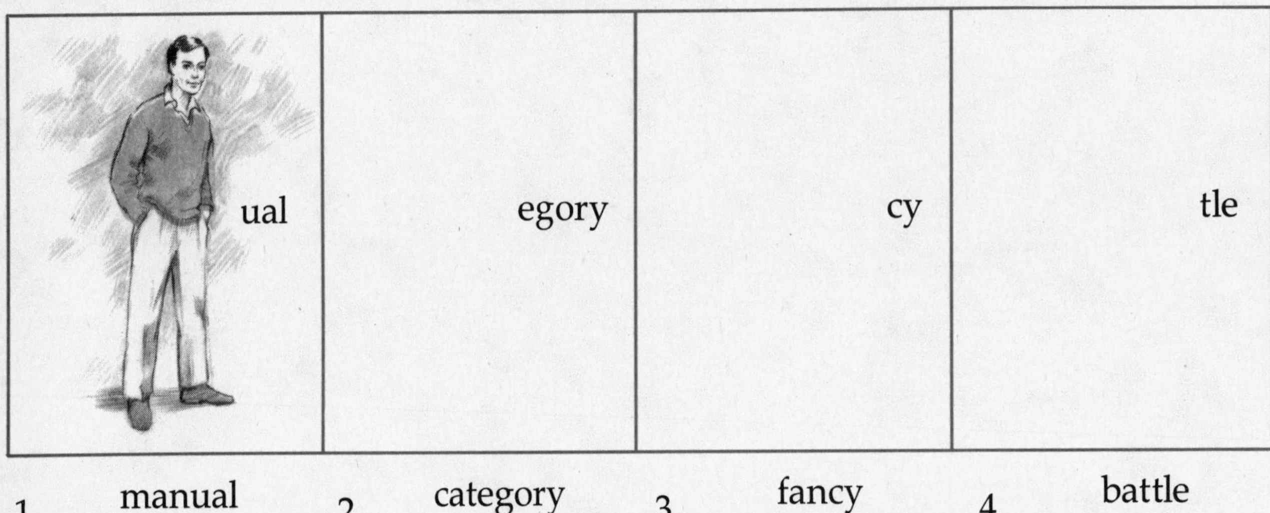

1. manual 2. category 3. fancy 4. battle

B. Underline five words in the paragraph below that you can picture. Then rewrite the paragraph using rebuses for those words.

Herb filled his cup with hot water from the teapot. Then he sat down to read the paper and enjoy his tea. When Herb took his first sip, he said, "Ugh!" He had forgotten to put a teabag into his cup.

Answers may vary.

Name

Teacher Note
Point out that on this page, words or syllables and pictures are used interchangeably. Pupils may wish to do their rebuses for part B on separate sheets of paper and hang them around the room.

If you have ever placed a classified ad in the newspaper, you know that it costs more money to show a longer ad. Many people shorten, or abbreviate, longer words in these ads. For example, **CA** is used to mean central air-conditioning. You probably won't find most of these abbreviations in a dictionary. Read the ads below and try to guess the meaning of each abbreviation. Then rewrite the ads, using the correct spelling of each word.

1.

> Hse for sale; 2 bdrms, ba, kit, dng rm; lrg porch & bk yd; wood w/ brk trim.

House for sale; two bedrooms, bath, kitchen, dining room; large porch and back yard;
wood with brick trim

2.

> Apt. for rent w/ dbl gar & sw pool; CA; 3 BR, 2 BA; Kit-Din area; Bsmt; wlk-in clst.

Apartment for rent with double garage and swimming pool; central air-conditioning;
three bedrooms, two baths; kitchen-dining room area; basement; walk-in closet

Name ______

Teacher Note
Tell pupils that abbreviations are a shortened form for words or names. You might wish to have pupils consult a local newspaper to see what abbreviations it uses in its classified section.

Each pair of thermometers below has a numeral beside it. The first numeral stands for a temperature on the Celsius scale. Use a red pencil to show how far the mercury must rise to reach that temperature. The second thermometer in each pair has a numeral which stands for the same temperature on the Fahrenheit scale. Use a blue pencil to show the mercury on that thermometer.

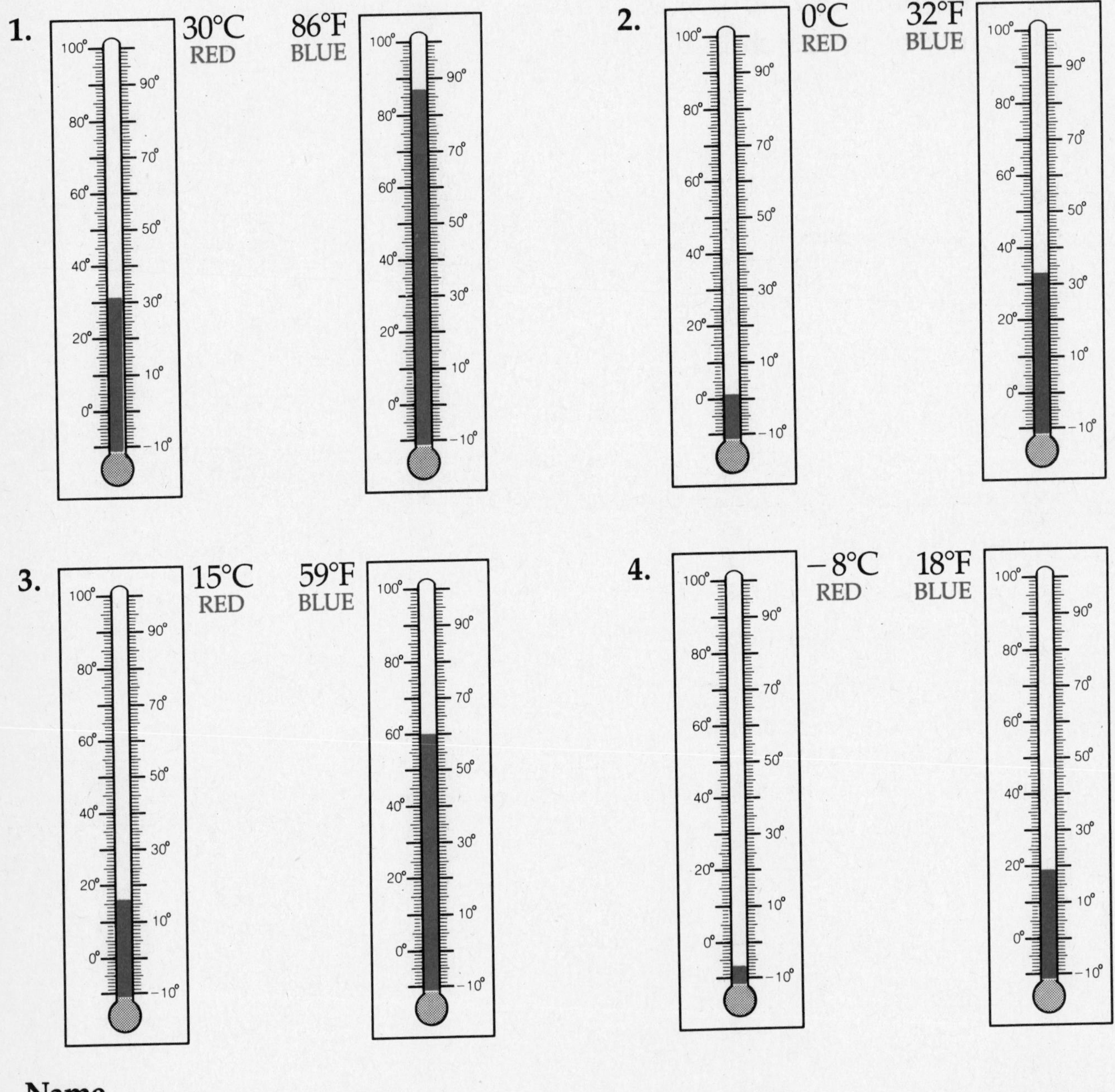

Name

Teacher Note
Tell the class that Celsius and Fahrenheit are different scales for measuring the same thing. Have pupils complete the page. Then play a game based on the two temperature scales. Ask pupils if they could swim when it was 30° Celsius, for example. Have pupils use the thermometers they marked to help them determine the answer.

Planning Projects

When you plan a project, you collect the tools or equipment you will need, decide on the goals you want to achieve, and make a plan of action to follow.

Read the activities below and put checks before the answers you choose. Each question has more than one correct answer.

1. Your teacher has asked your class to make posters which show the effects (results) of air pollution. Which of the following things will students need to make posters? Answers may vary.

   __√__ colored markers　_____ rulers　__√__ paints

   _____ encyclopedia　_____ tape recorder　_____ yarn

   __√__ poster paper　__√__ brushes　__√__ pencils

2. Suppose you are one of the three judges in a contest to decide who is the fastest runner in your class. Which of the following things will be most helpful in deciding the winner?

   __√__ a tape measure to judge the distance by

   __√__ a stopwatch to time the race

   _____ a book about running

3. You are going to a department store to buy gifts for the holidays. Which things would be the most useful?

   __√__ a shopping list of names and possible gifts

   __√__ money

   __√__ comfortable shoes for walking

   _____ an address book

   _____ stamps

Name ______________________________

Teacher Note
The answers pupils offer on this page may vary according to their experience. Discuss why some choices are more useful than others for conducting each project. Mention that this page deals only with the collecting of equipment for a project; there are other steps involved.

SKILL 26 Planning Projects

Read the story below and complete the activity following it.

World Biker

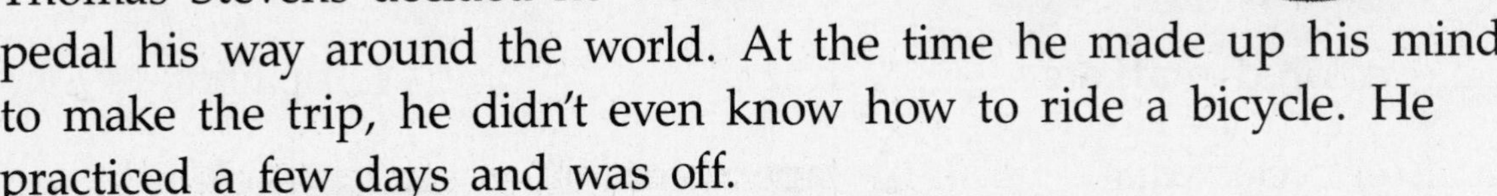

In the 1880s the bicycle had a large wheel in front and a tiny one in the back. The thing was difficult to ride in the city and almost impossible in the country.

In spite of the poor bicycle, Thomas Stevens decided he would pedal his way around the world. At the time he made up his mind to make the trip, he didn't even know how to ride a bicycle. He practiced a few days and was off.

He began in San Francisco in April 1884. In August, after 5000 kilometers of rough road and trouble, he arrived in Boston. There, he persuaded a bicycle manufacturer to pay for the rest of his trip.

Then Stevens sailed across the ocean and rode through Europe. By the time he got to Asia, he was loaded down with gifts.

By January 1887, Stevens was back in San Francisco and still had his bicycle! He was famous by that time. After that he made money giving lectures.

Suppose you were going on a bicycle trip around the world. Which things listed below would you consider necessary to take with you? Write **1** for those you think more necessary and **2** for those that are less necessary. Leave the line blank if you don't think the item is important at all.

Answers will vary.

_____ toothbrush _____ maps _____ medicines

_____ money _____ helmet _____ soap and towel

_____ backpack _____ blanket _____ tent

_____ extra clothes _____ pen and paper _____ goggles

_____ bicycle tools _____ food _____ water canteen

Name ______________________________

Teacher Note
After pupils complete the page, examine their various responses and use them as a starting point for a discussion on needs and wants. Point out that people's needs and wants can vary and that their priorities are therefore different.

Planning Projects

The students in the school patrol decided to go to Washington, D.C., for their year-end trip. They made this list of things to do before going on the trip. Decide on the 10 things which you think are the most important as they plan their project. Number the steps **1** to **10** to show in what order they should be done. Answers will vary.

_____ 1. Raise money for the trip.

_____ 2. Get parental permission slips to go on the trip.

_____ 3. Decide when to go.

_____ 4. Decide on the length of the trip.

_____ 5. Make travel arrangement plans.

_____ 6. Make housing and eating arrangements.

_____ 7. Plan recreation for free time in Washington.

_____ 8. Decide which clothes are needed for the trip.

_____ 9. Read up on some of the things to see and do in Washington.

_____ 10. Decide whether the students will be required to write about the trip after they return.

_____ 11. Decide how much spending money to take.

_____ 12. Plan the number of adults who will be invited to go along.

_____ 13. Decide whether to use a buddy system.

_____ 14. Plan whether or not cameras will be taken.

_____ 15. Decide how to pack the suitcases.

_____ 16. Estimate the cost of the whole trip after checking the cost of each part.

Name ________________________________

Teacher Note
Again, pupils may have different priorities for a class trip. When the pages are complete, check to see if there is a consensus on any items. Then use those as a base for coming up with a class list of 10 important items. Have pupils work together to number these in the order they should be accomplished.

Planning Projects

Read the story and answer the question.

Marilu and her grandpa wanted to build a birdhouse for the chickadees that came calling. They knew a small house would be good for the chickadees, but they wanted the house to be just right.

They went to the library and found a book that told how to make the birdhouse. It told them what size board to use. Then it told them how large to make the hole for the chickadee and how high the hole should be from the floor of the birdhouse. The book told them they needed a long pole to put the birdhouse on, so it would be away from danger on the ground.

Marilu and Grandpa also asked the advice of Mr. Lopez, who had built two birdhouses. He said to be sure the birdhouse could be opened so that it could be cleaned. He offered to lend them his saw, a hammer, and some nails for the project.

Marilu and Grandpa had fun making the birdhouse. Now they enjoy watching the chickadees come and go from their new home.

What did Marilu and Grandpa do that helped them to successfully build the birdhouse?

Answers will vary.

Marilu and Grandpa planned ahead. They did research to find out exactly what to do. They found out what materials and tools they would need to do the work. They also asked for advice from someone who had built two birdhouses.

Name ____________________

Teacher Note
Discuss the answers in class. Then have groups of pupils work together to think of a project they might want to do. Have them tell how they would plan for it.

Building Hypotheses

A **hypothesis** is an explanation of why something may have happened. A hypothesis is built upon facts that are given to you. Sometimes the same set of facts can lead to different hypotheses.

Below each story are three hypotheses that explain why the situation in the story may have happened. Read the story. Then put a check before the most likely hypothesis. Then, on the writing lines, give still another hypothesis of your own. Answers will vary.

1. One summer night, Jeff left his bicycle out in the front yard. The next morning, he found that his bicycle was all wet.

_____ a. It rained during the night.

_____ b. The evening dew made the grass and the bicycle wet.

_____ c. The bicycle was parked near a lawn sprinkler that had been left on all night.

____

____

2. Tina and Alex discovered that the library corner was in a mess. Some books were leaning on the shelves. Others had fallen to the floor.

_____ a. The children had been careless about putting books on the shelves. As a result, some books had fallen off.

_____ b. The books had not been neatly stacked in the beginning.

_____ c. The pegs which hold the bookshelf had slipped and caused the books to fall.

____

____

Name ____

Teacher Note
Explain that *hypothesis* is the singular form of *hypotheses*. Discuss pupils' responses to the situations on the page. Encourage pupils to defend the hypothesis they think is the most likely. Have them tell whether they think the hypotheses they write are as likely as those already given.

Building Hypotheses

Read each group of sentences. Answer the questions by writing your own hypothesis. Answers will vary.

1. Our basement is flooded. I think someone left the faucet on. What else could have caused the flooding?

   Possible: rain, broken pipe

2. When Pam and her friend came home from school yesterday, they noticed cars parked up and down both sides of the neighborhood street. Pam thought it might be a party, but the people looked unhappy. What else might have been happening?

   Possible: someone was ill, funeral, crisis meeting of neighborhood association

3. Ants keep coming into the kitchen. My parents think some jam or jelly is spilled in the back of a shelf. What else could account for the ants?

   Possible: an ant nest

4. Our rose bushes used to have big blooms. Now they just have little ones. Roberto thinks we didn't fertilize them. What other reason could there be?

   Possible: bugs, bad weather, not enough water

5. Hui says the dog is scratching itself all the time. Maybe the dog needs a bath. What else could cause the scratching?

   Possible: fleas

Name

Teacher Note
Pupils will probably suggest a variety of possibilities for the items on this page. Write their suggestions on the chalkboard and have the class number them as the most likely (*1*) to the least likely.

Building Hypotheses

A. Read the story. Then check the sentence that gives the most likely reason for what happened.

Randy was good at making fruit punches. One day she made a punch with grape juice. She added fresh fruit to the juice and served it to her friends. Everyone thought it was good. The next time Randy made a grape juice punch, she added sugar to the mixture. Her friends said the punch was too sweet. The third time that Randy made grape juice punch, she used fresh fruit and seltzer. Randy's friends liked this punch best of all.

Why was the second punch unsuccessful?

_____ Her friends liked the first punch better.

__✓__ The grape juice already had sugar in it.

_____ Randy's friends don't like sweet drinks.

_____ It didn't have seltzer in it.

B. How do you think that Randy could make another sweet punch which her friends would like? Write your ideas on the lines.

Answers will vary but should mention leaving out sugar.

____

____

____

Name ______________________________

Teacher Note
Caution pupils to read the story carefully before choosing a hypothesis. After pupils have completed the page, lead them in a discussion of why one hypothesis is better than the others.

Building Hypotheses

Read the paragraph. Then use clues to build a hypothesis.

Betsy has been gone from her room for a few minutes. She returns to find that the apple she left on her desk isn't there. Betsy sees some clues that might explain what happened to her apple.

1. Look at the picture. What clues do you see?

dog bone on desk; overturned desk lamp; dog burying something; wet weather outside; paw prints on carpet

2. What hypothesis might you build from these clues?

The dog took the apple and is burying it.

Name ______________________________

Teacher Note
Remind students that a hypothesis is a possible explanation of why something happened. Explain that sometimes there are clues that can lead to a hypothesis. Ask what pupils should do after forming a hypothesis.

Drawing Conclusions

Read each story. Then write a conclusion about how the trip will turn out. Tell why you think so.

1. Our class is going ice-skating on Sudbury Pond. We hope the ice is thick enough! Some of the students don't have skates, but they think they can borrow some. Janet says you're supposed to call the park department and get permission, so one of us will probably do that. We're wondering if we're allowed to have a bonfire to keep warm.

Conclusion The trip, if it happens at all, will be disorganized and not fun for everyone.

Why do you think so? The students don't know if the ice is thick, some students don't have skates, they haven't gotten permission, and they don't know the park rules.

2. Our class has planned a trip to the zoo to see how different animals are adapted to their homelands. We have arranged for a bus to take us there and back. We will each bring a bag lunch and will buy something to drink at a refreshment stand. We have each read about a different animal and will make a point of seeing that animal. Some of us are bringing cameras, and each of us will take notes.

Conclusion The trip will go smoothly; the students will accomplish their objectives.

Why do you think so? The students are organized and have made arrangements for food, transportation, and observation.

Name

Teacher Note
Review the definition of a *conclusion* with the class. Have pupils work on the page. Then discuss their conclusions and the reasons they offer for drawing them. Ask pupils which of the two trips described could be dangerous. Have pupils explain why.

Drawing Conclusions

Read each story. Then check the sentence under it that gives the best conclusion for each.

1. Leroy folded up the lawn chairs and put them in the shed. He brought the potted plants indoors. He also put the garbage cans in the garage. Leroy checked to make sure nothing else was loose in the yard. Then he went inside and listened once more to the reports on the radio.

_____ Leroy is going away on vacation.

__✓__ Leroy is expecting a big storm.

_____ Leroy has heard that a criminal is loose.

2. Miss Trinidad hunted all over the house. The longer she looked, the more upset she became and the more she squinted. Finally, in exasperation, she put her hand to her head. How Miss Trinidad smiled when she realized what a silly mistake she had made!

__✓__ Miss Trinidad found she was wearing her eyeglasses.

_____ Miss Trinidad's headache went away.

_____ Miss Trinidad realized she was wearing her missing ring.

3. Duncan got in the elevator and pushed the button. When the door opened, he trudged wearily to his apartment door. It took Duncan several minutes before he realized that his key just wouldn't fit into the lock. When he looked up, he saw why.

_____ Duncan had the wrong key.

_____ The lock on the door was broken.

__✓__ Duncan had gotten off at the wrong floor.

Name ______________________________

Teacher Note
Tell pupils to think of themselves as detectives as they work on this page. When the page is completed, discuss pupils' conclusions. Ask for volunteers to explain why each conclusion is more likely than the others. For example, in item 1 Leroy's preparations for a vacation probably would not include bringing the plants indoors.

Drawing Conclusions

Read each group of sentences that tells something about Theodore Roosevelt. Then answer the question about your conclusion.

1. Theodore Roosevelt, the 26th president of the United States, often used the word *bully*. When he was given permission to form the Rough Riders, a special army regiment, he said, "Bully!" Upon hearing that he had just been elected president by the greatest popular vote up to that time, he said, "That's bully!"

   What conclusion can you draw about Theodore Roosevelt's use of the word *bully?*

   Possible answers include: He used it when he received good news or when he was happy or pleased about something.

2. "You must control Alice," a man advised Roosevelt. "I can do one of two things," Theodore Roosevelt replied. "I can be President of the United States, or I can control my daughter Alice. I cannot possibly do both."

   What conclusion can you draw about Alice Roosevelt?

   Possible answers include: Alice had a mind of her own, and it was a full-time job to control her.

Name

Teacher Note
Have pupils give explanations for their conclusions. Then have them give brief descriptions about someone, real or imaginary, so their classmates may draw a conclusion about the person.

Look at the cards below.

Notice that only one card has a heart on it. If a friend were to turn all the cards face down and mix them up, you would have **one chance out of four** (one in four) of picking up the card with the heart on it. You can make this conclusion because only one of the four cards has a heart on it.

1. If you wanted to fix it so that your friend would have **one chance in three** of picking the card with a heart on it, how many cards of different suits would you place upside-down? three

2. If the cards below were turned face down and mixed up, what chance would you have of picking the card with two hearts on it?

   one chance in ten

Was your conclusion **one chance in ten**? That is correct.

3. Now decide what chance you would have of picking out the card with one heart if the cards below were turned upside-down and mixed up.

   one chance in eight

Name ______________________

Teacher Note
Explain that the law of chances is sometimes helpful in drawing conclusions. You might wish to have a deck of cards in the room when pupils do this page so they can try out the problems given and invent more of their own.

Proposing Alternatives

Before you solve a problem, you should think of several alternate ways to handle it and choose the best one. Read about the problems below. Check the alternative to handle each problem which you think is better than the others. Then, on the lines, write another good alternative. Answers will vary.

1. You are home alone in a first floor apartment. Suddenly, water starts dripping on you from the ceiling. The people who live upstairs are away on vacation. You should:

_____ call your parents at work and ask them what to do.

_____ find the building caretaker if you can.

_____ get a ladder and try to get into the upstairs apartment by opening an unlocked window.

____

____

2. You rode the bus to the shopping center on a rainy day. You spent all of your money on toys and food. Now it is time to go home and you have no money for bus fare. You should:

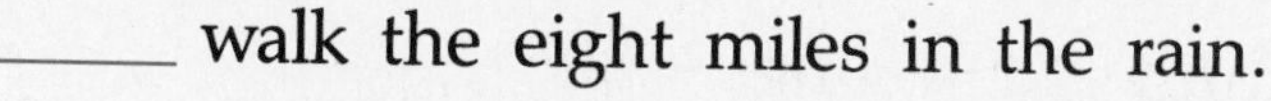

_____ walk the eight miles in the rain.

_____ go back to the store where you bought several toys and try to return one of them.

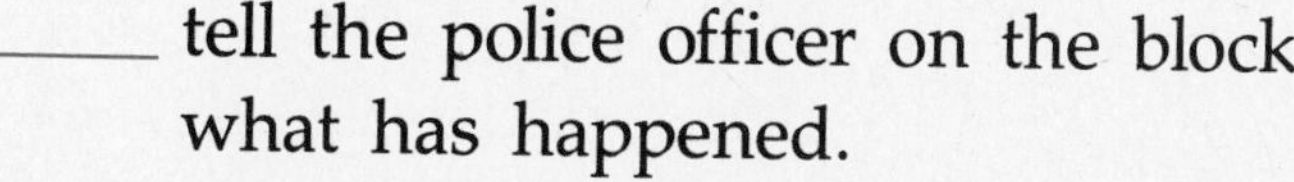

_____ tell the police officer on the block what has happened.

____

____

Name ____

Teacher Note
Before pupils begin this page, discuss the meaning of *alternate* and *alternative*. Tell pupils that there is no right or wrong answer to each problem on this page but that they should be prepared to defend their choices.

Proposing Alternatives

Read each story. Then write two ways that the person in the story might solve the problem.

A. Bill Johnson was worried as he walked home from school. Last week the teacher allowed Bill's friend Jack to change seats. Now, Jack sat directly behind Bill.

Jack's move caused a problem. Every few minutes, Jack leaned forward and whispered to Bill. Bill had trouble getting his work done.

Yesterday, the teacher talked about the science fair. Because Jack was whispering, Bill was not sure what the students were supposed to do.

1. Answers will vary. ______________________________

____

2. ______________________________

____

B. Georgia wanted a certain blue sweater for her birthday. Her older sister said she would buy it for Georgia. So Georgia described the sweater and told her sister where to get it. When her birthday came, Georgia eagerly opened her sister's present. Her sister watched in satisfaction. Imagine Georgia's surprise when the sweater in the box was not the one she wanted. Georgia knew her sister had gone to a lot of trouble and she didn't want to hurt her feelings; still, she was disappointed. She was not sure what to do.

1. Answers will vary. ______________________________

____

2. ______________________________

____

Name ______________________________

Teacher Note
Tell pupils that there are several ways to resolve each of the conflicts on the page. Their job is to propose two alternatives that they think make sense and be prepared to tell why. You might want to list on the chalkboard all the suggestions pupils make so they can see the scope of possible actions.

Proposing Alternatives

A. Your parents have given you permission to cut up some old magazines. How would you use magazines for the projects listed below? Write your ideas on the lines. Answers will vary.

1. For the bulletin board at school ____________________

2. For a written report ____________________

3. For a greeting card you'll make ____________________

4. In a booklet you want to assemble ____________________

B. Your grandmother has said you may have some of her old scraps of cloth. Tell how you would use them in the following projects: Answers will vary.

1. In an art project ____________________

2. In a sewing project ____________________

3. In a cleaning project ____________________

4. In a game ____________________

Name ____________________

Teacher Note
Encourage pupils to be original in their responses. Some pupils might enjoy demonstrating what they would do with one of the items. When pupils have completed the page, list their ideas on the chalkboard to demonstrate the wide variety of alternate actions.

Proposing Alternatives

A. Study each item pictured below. Then think of alternate ways to use it. Write your ideas on the lines. Answers will vary.

1.

2.

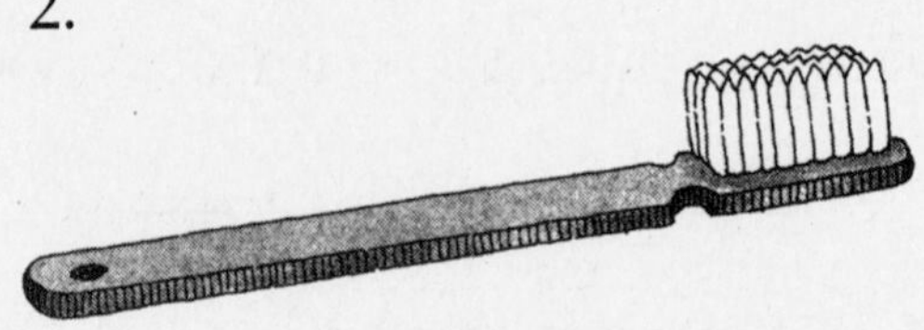

3.

4.

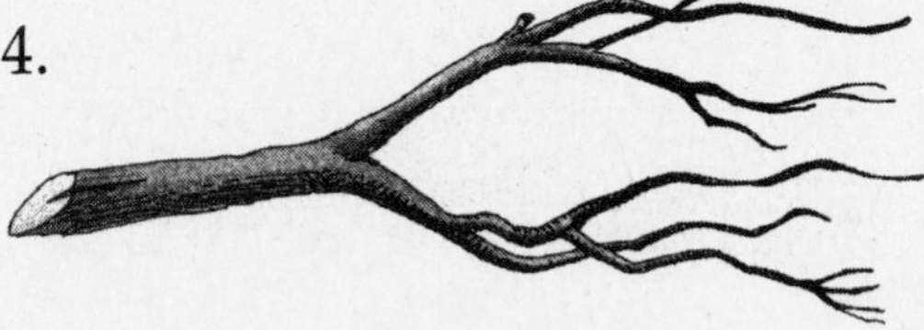

5.

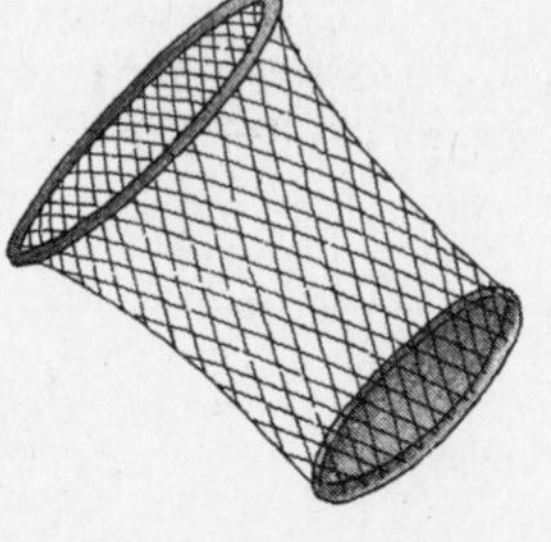

6.

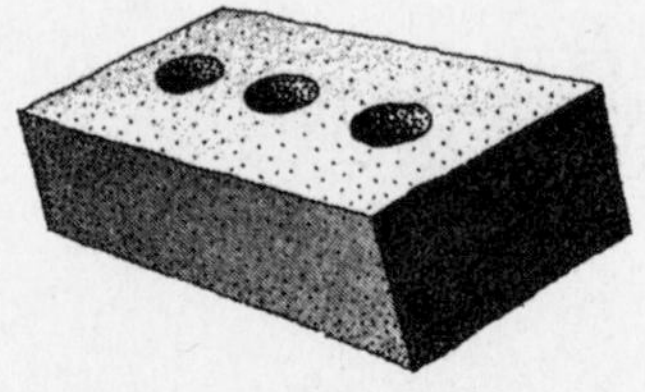

B. Think of a common item that you use all the time. Then draw a picture to show an alternate way of using that item.

Name

Teacher Note
This page calls for original thinking. Explain to the class that sometimes you have to stretch your mind to think of good alternatives while other times they are more obvious. Have pupils share their responses.

A. Planning Projects

To conduct a scientific project, a scientist follows certain steps. Study the comic strip below. Then write under each panel the correct step from the box.

4. Do the experiment.

6. Develop a conclusion.

1. Begin with the problem.

3. Collect the information you need.

5. Study the results.

2. Develop a hypothesis about how to solve it.

1. Begin with the problem.	4. Do the experiment.
2. Develop a hypothesis about how to solve it.	5. Study the results.
3. Collect the information you need.	6. Develop a conclusion.

Name ______________________

Teacher Note
After completing the page, pupils may discuss and check their work with you or a partner.

B. Building Hypotheses

Mr. Ramonte came into this room and took three things—a flower, some sheets of music, and his eyeglasses. Write a hypothesis to explain why. Use clues from the picture to help you.

Answers will vary.

Possible: Mr. Ramonte is a concert pianist and he is off to play in a concert.

C. Proposing Alternatives

The electricity has gone off in your house because of a storm. Write an alternate action for each of the following tasks. Answers may vary.

1. vacuuming the rug using carpet sweeper
2. mixing batter in the blender mixing by hand
3. watching television reading, playing game
4. ironing your clothes smoothing them, spreading them out to dry
5. turning on the air conditioner using a hand fan, opening window

Name ______________________

Teacher Note
After completing the page, pupils may discuss and check their work with you or a partner.

UNIT 6

Evaluating

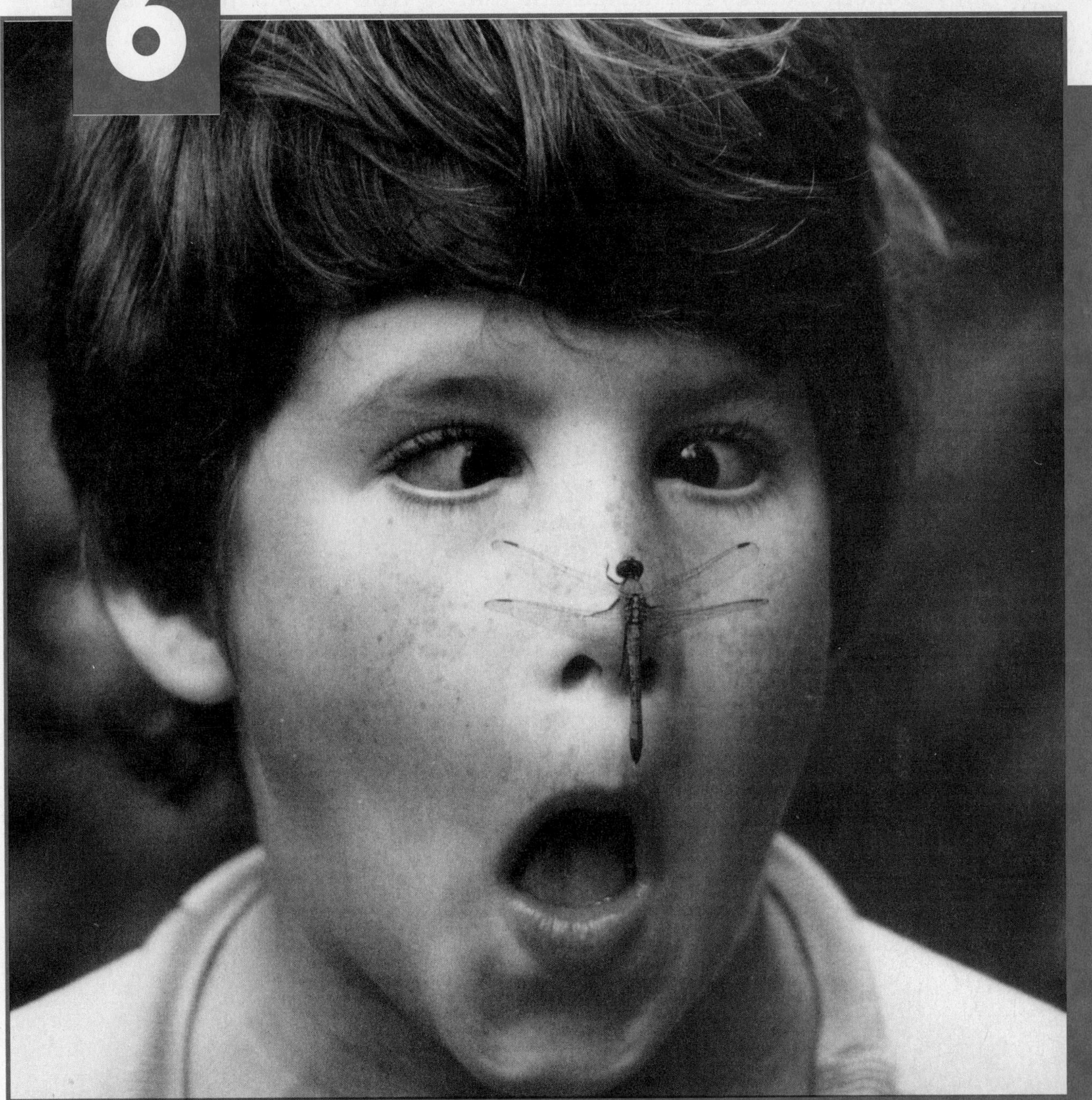

Teacher Note
In order to develop Bloom's sixth stage—evaluating—the pupil needs to engage in the following skills:
- Testing Generalizations
- Developing Criteria
- Judging Accuracy
- Making Decisions
- Identifying Values
- Interpreting Mood of a Story

Evaluating means making a judgment or decision about something. What is happening in the picture? What does the boy's expression tell you? Did he expect the dragonfly to land on his nose? How do you know? Would you like to have the same thing happen to you? Why or why not?

Testing Generalizations

A good **generalization** is a statement that is true for all the details that lead up to it.

A. Read each statement and the words which follow. If the statement is true for **all** of the words, write **T** on the line. If the statement is not true about **one** of the words, write **F** on the line.

__T__ 1. These items can be used to tie something.
rope string ribbon cord wire

__F__ 2. These animals are covered with feathers.
chicken robin ostrich peacock dolphin

__T__ 3. These are different kinds of workers.
teacher writer electrician carpenter florist

__F__ 4. These articles can be found in a kitchen.
refrigerator cabinets dishes car stove

B. Three meanings are given for each word below. If all three meanings are correct for the word, write **T** on the line. If only two of the meanings are correct, write **F** on the line. You may use a dictionary.

__T__ 1. **chest:** a part of the body; a box with a lid; a piece of furniture.

__F__ 2. **seal:** to close tightly; a sea animal; a gumdrop

__T__ 3. **shower:** a kind of bath; a party for someone; light rain

__T__ 4. **tied:** fastened; made the same score as someone else; arranged in a knot or bow

Name ____________________

Teacher Note
Review the definition of a *generalization* with the class. Then have pupils complete the page. Discuss their answers and why they do or do not fit the generalization given. For example, in item 2 (part A), a dolphin does not have feathers, so the generalization is not true.

SKILL 30 Testing Generalizations

Read the story below and complete the activity that follows it.

Dinosaur footprints are a rare sight to many people. However, near Price, Utah, they are very common. Dinosaurs walked in the soft sand and clay of eastern Utah millions of years ago. Their footprints are found in the coal mines in the area.

There are large prints which were left by an adult tyrannosaurus, and small prints left by a young one. Right down the middle of both footprints are marks left by the big tail of the adult and the tiny tail of the smaller one.

The prints of the meat-eating tyrannosaurus and the plant-eating brontosaurus are so common in Price that many residents walk by them every day without noticing them.

Copy the words that make each sentence an accurate generalization.

1. The area where Price, Utah, is now located was once
   - a. very dangerous.
   - b. full of dinosaurs.

   full of dinosaurs.

2. The tyrannosaurus and the brontosaurus
   - a. did not like the same food.
   - b. ate green plants.

   did not like the same food.

3. The dinosaurs left footprints because
   - a. the clay and sand were soft.
   - b. the ground was wet.

   the clay and sand were soft.

4. Dinosaur footprints around Price, Utah, are
   - a. like those in most towns.
   - b. unique to that area.

   unique to that area.

Name ______________________

Teacher Note
Pupils should be able to complete this page independently. Ask the class to think of additional generalizations they might make based on the story. For example, most Americans do not usually see dinosaur footprints.

Testing Generalizations

Each of these generalizations states something that is not always true. Write a sentence of your own to prove that the generalization is not always true.

Answers will vary.

Example: All animals on a farm are raised for food.
A farm dog is a pet.

1. All basketball players are over six feet tall.

____

2. All people who own cars know how to drive.

____

3. Parties are always fun.

____

4. Flowers bloom only in spring and summer.

____

5. All television shows are violent.

____

Name ______________________________

Teacher Note
Explain to the class that *false generalizations* can mislead people. Tell pupils that their task on this page is to disprove each generalization given. They can use personal experience or look up information, such as the height of a relatively short professional or collegiate basketball player, to prove that the generalization is not always true.

Developing Criteria

A **criterion** is a rule, or guideline, that you use for judging something. (The plural of **criterion** is **criteria**.)

A. Your family has told you that you can have a new pet. Here are the criteria your family has given:

- The pet must be small enough to keep indoors.
- The pet must be intelligent enough to follow commands.
- The pet must be useful to the family in some way.

1. Circle the animal that you would choose on the basis of the criteria.
   Answers will vary, but most students will choose the dog.
2. Tell why you circled that animal.
   Answers will vary, but students should show how criteria were met.

B. You are going to learn how to play a musical instrument. These are your criteria:

- You want to be able to play it in a band.
- You want it to be in the brass family.
- You want something that isn't too heavy to hold.

1. Circle the instrument that you would choose on the basis of the criteria.
2. Tell why you circled that instrument.
   Students should point out that the trumpet meets the criteria best.

Name ______________________

Teacher Note
Explain that *criteria* are guidelines that people follow or use as a measure. Point out that your school has a set of criteria for grading report cards. Have pupils complete the page and then defend their answers by measuring them against the criteria given.

Developing Criteria

Suppose that your class is going to have a science fair. You need to develop some criteria for this event. Your class has agreed that there will be entrance requirements about who can take part. There will also be requirements for the way the exhibits are set up. On the lines below, make a list of criteria that you think would be useful for a good class science fair.

1. Answers will vary. ______________________________

____

2. ______________________________

____

3. ______________________________

____

4. ______________________________

____

5. ______________________________

____

Name ______________________________

Teacher Note
Before pupils work independently on this page, you might want to have a general discussion about a class science fair. You might also want to treat this page as a class project and complete it orally. If not, have pupils share their ideas when all the pages have been done. At that point some pupils may wish to revise their criteria.

SKILL 32 Judging Accuracy

When you read or listen, ask yourself if what is written or said makes sense. Sometimes people say one thing and then another that is just the opposite. It is difficult to determine what they really mean.

Read these paragraphs. Find the sentences in each that **contradict**, or say the opposite thing. Underline these contradictory sentences.

1. The first known crossword puzzle appeared in the year 1913. It ran in a newspaper called the **New York World**. An editor of the paper, Arthur Wynne, made up the puzzle. It had 32 words and was in the shape of a diamond. No one is sure who wrote the puzzle.

2. The **New York World** was also a leader when it came to the nation's first comic strip. In 1893 the newspaper published a full color comic called "Hogan's Alley." It introduced a set of humorous characters to the paper's readers. The colorless page was not very funny. The public soon cried for more.

3. William Randolph Hearst published a comic strip called "The Yellow Kid" in his paper, the **Morning-Journal**. This was the first comic to use speech balloons for dialogue. It is not known who the publisher of the newspaper was.

Name ______________________________

Teacher Note
Caution pupils to read each paragraph on the page carefully before they attempt to determine which sentence contradicts another. Once pupils have finished the page, discuss the contradictory sentences.

Judging Accuracy

Sometimes when people speak or write, they are not exact in the words that they use. This makes it hard to understand just what they mean. You cannot make good judgments about things if you do not know what is really meant.

Read the paragraph. Find five examples of a word or phrase that is not exact. Underline these examples. Then rewrite the paragraph using more exact words for those that you underlined.

The wind blew a lot. The sky was darkish. Some clouds were sort of moving in our direction. We were kind of worried. Things did not seem so good.

Paragraphs will vary.

Name ____________________

Teacher Note
Before pupils rewrite the paragraph, be sure they have correctly identified the vague, inexact words. Have pupils share their finished paragraphs with the class.

Judging Accuracy

When you judge something, you come to a conclusion about it. It is important that your conclusions make sense. When you make a conclusion, base it on the facts that are given.

Read the two paragraphs. Underline the concluding sentence in each paragraph. Then circle the conclusion that does not follow the facts given.

Carmen slowed down and tried to calm herself as she approached Fred's yard. She smiled weakly at Fred's dog, Romp, when he barked at her. Then, she walked as quickly as she could up to the door and rang the bell. When Romp followed her and tried to lick her hand, Carmen jumped and pulled it away. Carmen did not like Romp.

Carmen slowed down and tried to calm herself as she approached Fred's yard. She smiled weakly at Fred's dog, Romp, when he barked at her. Then, she walked as quickly as she could up to the door and rang the bell. When Romp followed her and tried to lick her hand, Carmen jumped and pulled it away. Carmen was afraid of Romp.

Reread the sentence that you circled. In your own words, write why this conclusion does not make sense with the facts given.

Students should point out that Carmen smiled at the dog but otherwise acted afraid by trying to calm herself, walking quickly, and jumping when Romp tried to lick her hand.

Name ____________________

Teacher Note
Tell pupils to read the two paragraphs closely before deciding on the best conclusion. Ask pupils to share their reasons for choosing the second paragraph conclusion as the most likely. Discuss how Carmen might have acted if the other conclusion (she did not like Romp) were true.

SKILL 32 Judging Accuracy

When you write a report, you get information from different sources. It is important to make good choices about the sources you use.

Read the paragraph below. Then fill in each blank with one of the sources given in the box. Choose the best source for each sentence.

globe	encyclopedia	poem	chart
newspaper	dictionary	television	interpreter

From looking at a ___globe___, you can tell that China has many neighbors. According to a current ___encyclopedia___, only one other country in the world has more land than China. That country is Canada.

On a ___chart___ showing world population, you can see that China has more people than any other nation. China also has the world's oldest living civilization. A recent program on ___television___ showed that the Chinese were the first people to develop the compass, paper, silk, and fine china. China also has an old and great body of literature and painting. Many of the paintings are a kind of fine handwriting called **calligraphy**. The ___dictionary___ says that it is pronounced **kə lĭg′ rə fē**. This ancient art is still practiced today.

鮮
桂
滕

Name ______________________________

Teacher Note
Stress that pupils should choose the best or most likely source for each blank. Discuss other sources of information that pupils might use in research (almanacs, atlases, textbooks, and so on).

SKILL 33 Making Decisions

There are often many ways to do something. Some ways are better than others. It is a good idea to stop and think about all the possibilities before you decide.

Each sentence tells about what someone wants to do. The three sentences that follow give ways that this could be done. Underline the sentence that you think tells the best way. Answers may vary.

1. Nora doesn't have enough money to buy flowers for the table of a fall party she is giving.

   a. She could use a green houseplant.
   b. She could use autumn leaves.
   c. She could make a centerpiece.

2. Jim wants to remember to call his grandmother on a certain date to wish her a happy birthday.

   a. He could tie a string around his finger.
   b. He could mark the date on a calendar.
   c. He could write a note to himself and put it in a place he always looks.

3. Nigel wants to buy a used bicycle.

   a. He could ask his friends if they want to sell theirs.
   b. He could check the local classified ads for bicycles.
   c. He could ask at the bike shop to see if they have any.

4. Brett wants to find an original way to thank his neighbor for a weekend at the seashore.

   a. He could write a thank-you note.
   b. He could go over and thank the neighbor in person.
   c. He could give the neighbor a scrapbook of photos he took during the weekend.

Name ______________________________

Teacher Note
After pupils complete the page, discuss the answers given and those that pupils selected. Ask the class to think of at least one more possible solution for each problem. Stress that there is not necessarily only one way to solve these problems.

Making Decisions

Read the sentences. Each tells about what someone wants to do. Decide what you think is the best way to solve the problem. Write your idea on the lines. Answers will vary.

1. Yuri accidently got locked out of his house. No one else is home. Yuri is upset because he has a lot of homework to complete as well as a test to study for. What should Yuri do?

____

____

2. Maggie went to the store to buy a few groceries for her mother. At the checkout counter, she realized that she had far too much to carry home. What should Maggie do?

____

____

3. Ray looks out the window and sees fresh-fallen snow on the ground one morning. He wants to share the beauty of this with his pen pal in Hawaii who has never seen snow. What should Ray do?

____

____

Name ______________________________

Teacher Note
After pupils complete the page, discuss their resolutions. You might want to suggest that pupils role play some of the situations and possible solutions.

Making Decisions

Read each story and answer the question.

1. Tomorrow Nathan would fly his kite in the kite-flying contest. While eating dinner, he remembered his kite was outside. He decided that he'd get it after he finished dinner. Then he noticed there were dark clouds in the sky, and it was very windy. Nathan decided not to wait. He went outside and got the kite. The next day Nathan won the kite-flying contest.

How might the story have ended if Nathan had made a different decision? Answers will vary.

2. Samantha had planned to practice her jumps for the ice show, especially the last, most difficult one. Her friends were going to a new movie, and she decided to go with them instead. At the ice show the next day, she performed her jumps well, except for the last one. She made a bad landing and fell to the ice.

How might the story have ended if Samantha had made a different decision?

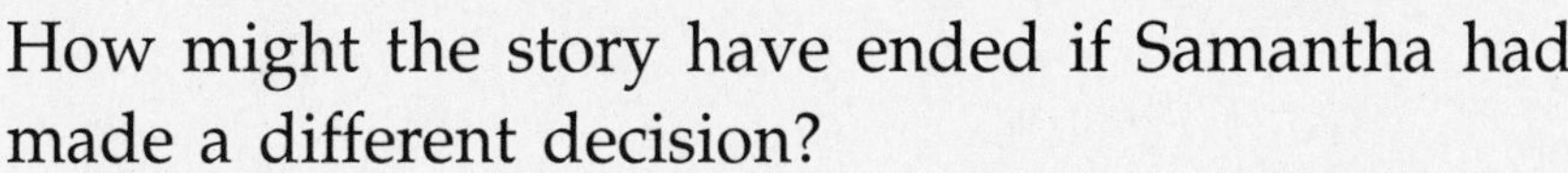

Answers will vary.

Name

Teacher Note
Point out that Samantha still might have fallen even if she had practiced, but the practice might have helped. Then ask volunteers to tell about a decision they made that affected the outcome of a situation.

SKILL 33

Making Decisions

Read the paragraphs. Put a check by the decision you would make. Then explain why you made that decision.

You live in Australia, where there are many kangaroos. You've seen kangaroos leap as high as six feet (1.8 m) and hop at speeds up to 40 miles (64.4 km) per hour.

You decide to care for a baby kangaroo, called a joey, whose mother was killed. You get a permit to care for a wild animal. Then you find out how to take care of the joey and what it will need.

As the joey grows under your care, it becomes a member of your family and is very tame. However, by the time it is one year old, it can live very well on its own. Now you must make a decision. You want to do what is best for the kangaroo. What should you do?

Answers will vary.

1. _____ Get a permit so the kangaroo can stay with you longer.

   _____ Return the kangaroo to the wild.

   _____ Take the kangaroo to a nature preserve for wild animals.

2. Why do you think you made the best decision?

   Answers will vary.
   ____
   ____
   ____
   ____

Name ____

Teacher Note
Pupils may make different choices. Discuss what a nature preserve is. Point out that the kangaroo will need room to jump and hop. It may need protection from hunters and animal predators because it is tame and might not be afraid of them. Encourage pupils to explain their answers.

SKILL 34 Identifying Values

Values are standards of behavior that people feel are important.

A. Some values—words and their definitions—are listed in the box. Below the list are five sentences that give examples of people living by these values. On the line following each sentence, write which value is being shown.

courtesy	kindness, respect for others
courage	meeting danger and bad times bravely
affection	love, friendship
rectitude	honesty, fair play

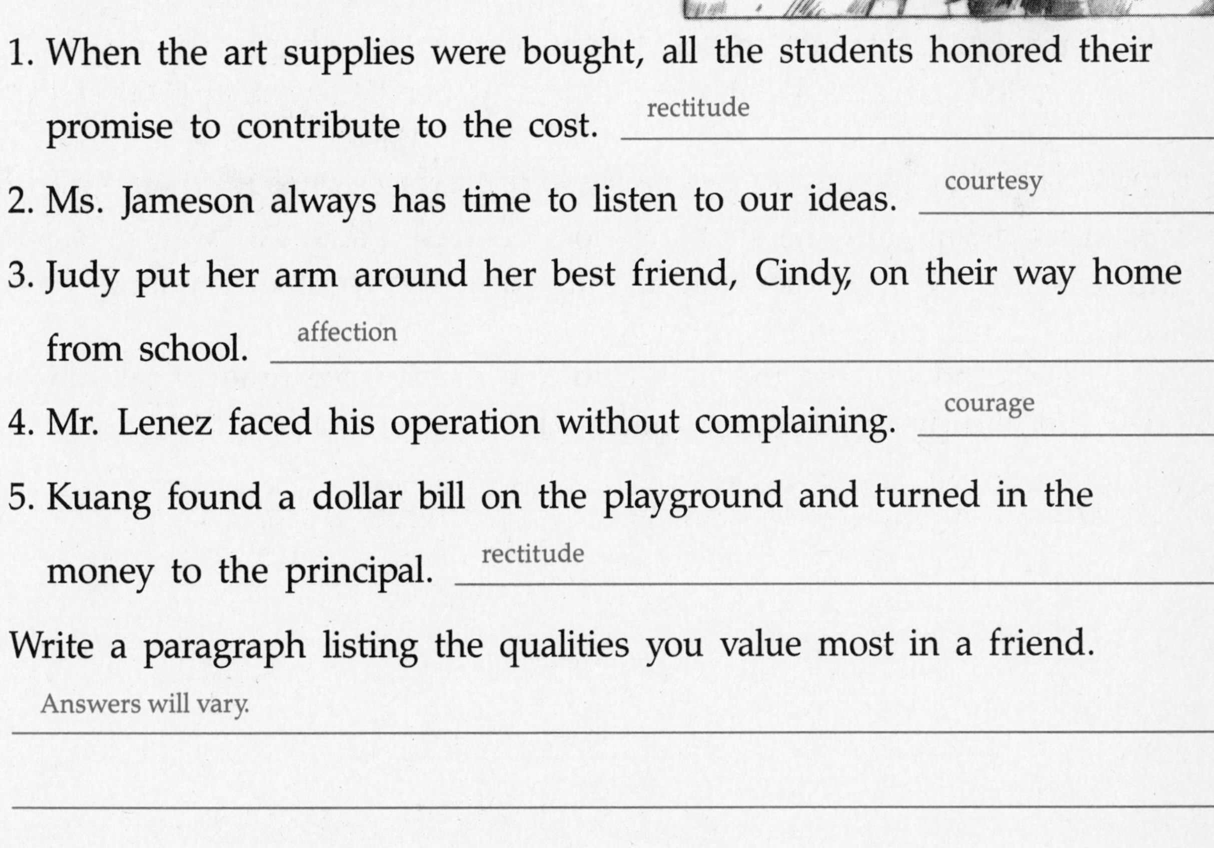

1. When the art supplies were bought, all the students honored their promise to contribute to the cost. rectitude
2. Ms. Jameson always has time to listen to our ideas. courtesy
3. Judy put her arm around her best friend, Cindy, on their way home from school. affection
4. Mr. Lenez faced his operation without complaining. courage
5. Kuang found a dollar bill on the playground and turned in the money to the principal. rectitude

B. Write a paragraph listing the qualities you value most in a friend.

Answers will vary.

Name ______________________

Teacher Note
You might begin by discussing some of the values held by your community, school, and so on. After pupils complete the page, have them share their answers to part B. List on the chalkboard all the qualities that pupils value in a friend.

Identifying Values

Read the story. Then write three things you think Trudy might do. Check the one you think she **should** do.

Trudy selected a fancy pen and some greeting cards at the card shop. She got in line to pay for her things. When it was her turn, Trudy put her purchases on the counter. The woman behind Trudy put her things on the counter, too. Trudy noticed that the woman was buying a cute notepad. She wished she had enough money to get one.

While Trudy was getting out her money, the clerk put her things in a bag. Trudy paid, thanked the clerk, and left. When she got home, Trudy found that the clerk had put the notepad in her bag with her other things by mistake.

"Maybe the clerk wanted you to have it," said Trudy's brother. "You did want it, and I'm sure the shop has lots of these pads. Anyway, it wasn't **your** mistake. Why should you have to go to the trouble of taking it back? They might not believe you!"

Trudy wanted to keep the pad, and she didn't have time to take it back today. Still, Trudy wasn't sure what to do. Answers will vary. Possible:

1. Trudy could call the store, explain the mistake, and make plans to return the notepad.

2. Trudy could ask her parents to take it back.

3. Trudy could call the woman if she knows her and give it back.

Name ______________________________

Teacher Note
Have pupils complete the page. Then discuss all the possible ways to resolve the situation. List pupils' ideas on the chalkboard. Ask pupils to explain why they checked one idea rather than the others. Discuss the arguments that Trudy's brother brought up and how Trudy could respond to them.

Mood of a Story

Part of the **mood** of a story is based on the feelings of the characters.

Read each paragraph. Make each sentence in parentheses correct by circling the word that shows what the character is feeling.

"Ay, ay!" groaned Little Turtle. He was thinking about his father, Big Wolf. Big Wolf was not pleased with Little Turtle. (Little Turtle was: **hopeful**, **worried**, **carefree**.)

Little Turtle hung his head. He would have to tell Big Wolf the reason why he was late. He had been grinding corn for his grandmother. (Little Turtle was: **tired**, **contented**, **sad**.)

He loved his grandmother. She was gentle and wise. She was the best teller of tales in the whole village. But Big Wolf never seemed to understand all this. (Little Turtle was: **happy**, **foolish**, **disappointed**.)

"So that is why you are late!" Big Wolf exclaimed. "You can find time to work for others, but you do not do your own work." (Big Wolf was: **friendly**, **angry**, **calm**.)

Just then a woman ran up to Big Wolf and cried, "My small child is lost in the desert. No one has found her. I fear for my child's safety." (The woman was: **concerned**, **doubtful**, **grateful**.)

Little Turtle was alarmed. The child could not live long in the hot desert without water. He ran off to find her. (Little Turtle was: **mad**, **confused**, **courageous**.)

Little Turtle returned some time later with the lost child. Then Big Wolf said to him, "I see you are wiser than I am in some ways. You know that helping others is sometimes more important than helping yourself." (Big Wolf was: **unfair**, **kind**, **proud**.)

Name ______________________

Teacher Note
Have pupils complete the page independently. Then, as you discuss each answer, ask pupils to explain how they were able to determine the character's mood. You might also ask them to think of other words to describe the character's feelings in each instance.

Mood of a Story

A story's mood can be created by the setting, or where the story takes place.

Read the paragraph. Then answer the questions.

The waves pounded the shore, bringing the ocean a little closer to Buzz with each new onslaught. He watched as the white froth eddied around his sand castle, then reluctantly dropped back, only to return seconds later with the next wave. It was too cold to swim today and too rough. Yet Buzz thought these gray, windy days at the beach were the best of all. It was then, he felt, that the ocean really showed its strength. As another wave broke away part of the castle, Buzz shivered. It was comforting to know that he was here on the shore, not far from the cottage, and not out at sea where the waves ruled unchallenged. Answers may vary.

1. How would you describe the place where Buzz is? ______________

   windswept ocean beach with sand near summer homes

2. What kind of day is it? cloudy, windy

3. How does Buzz feel? excited, a little fearful, glad to be safe on shore, awed

Name ______________

Teacher Note
Review the meaning of *setting*. Then allow pupils to work independently. When you discuss pupils' answers, also discuss how the setting helps create the mood of the story.

A. Developing Criteria

Study each picture and the information that goes with it. Then answer the question.

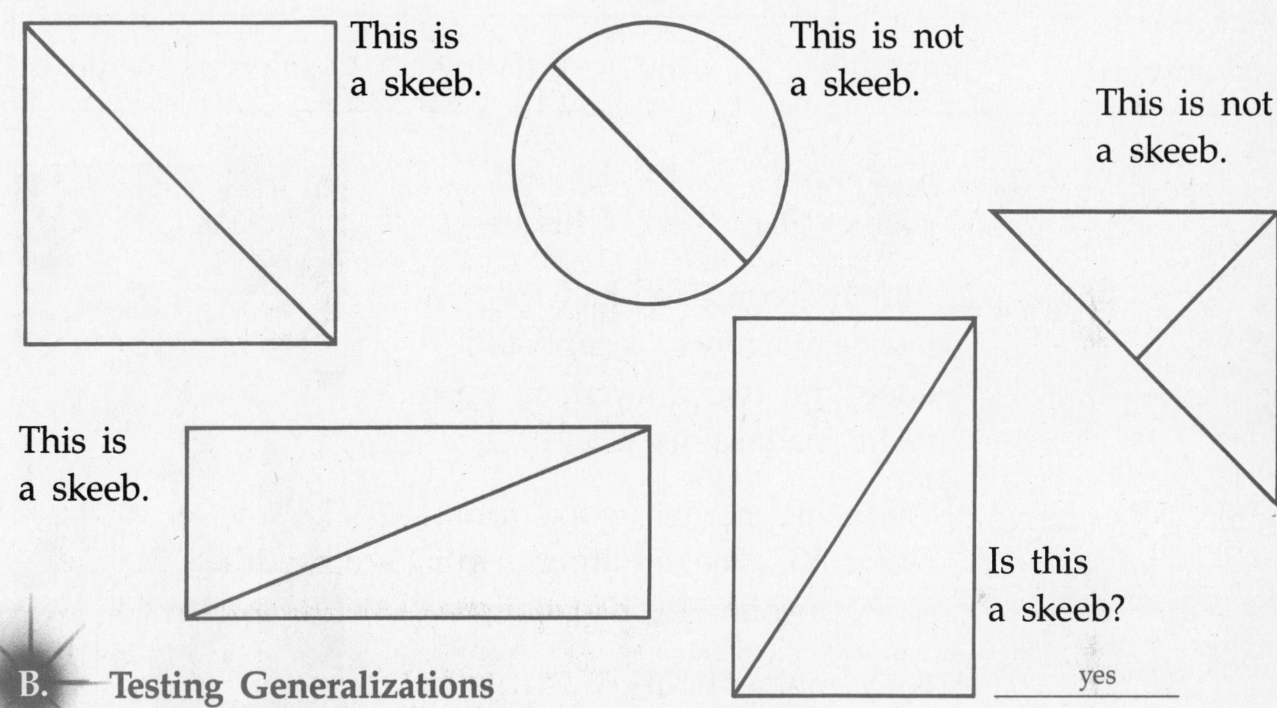

yes

B. Testing Generalizations

If the generalization about skeebs is true, write **true**. If the generalization is not true, write **false**.

1. Skeebs must have four sides. true
2. A skeeb can be a circle. false
3. A skeeb must be a square. false
4. All skeebs have a diagonal line dividing them into two equal parts.

   true

5. Skeebs must have only straight lines. true

Name ______________________________

Teacher Note
After completing the page, pupils may discuss and check their work with you or a partner.

C. Mood of a Story

Read each sentence of the story. Choose a word from the box that best fits the emotion or action of the character. Write the word on the line.

confused	thoughtless	silly	happy	guilty	angry

happy 1. Kirk raced into the kitchen, singing at the top of his lungs.

thoughtless 2. Within seconds he had the refrigerator door, a cupboard door, and two drawers all open as he made himself a snack.

guilty 3. When his mother's good dish broke, Kirk looked around to see if anyone else had noticed.

confused 4. For a moment Kirk wasn't sure just what to do.

D. Identifying Values

Write a paragraph in which you tell Kirk what to do.

Answers will vary.

Name

Teacher Note
After completing the page, pupils may discuss and check their work with you or a partner.